A CROWN OF BEAUTY

The Bahá'í Faith and the Holy Land

Written by

EUNICE BRAUN

Concept and Design by

HUGH E. CHANCE

GEORGE RONALD

OXFORD

First published by
George Ronald
46 High Street, Kidlington, Oxford, OX5 2DN

© Eunice Braun and Hugh E. Chance
1982
Reprinted 1987, 1992

ISBN 0 85398 139 6 (cased)
ISBN 0 85398 140 X (paper)

Photographs
A. L. Thompson – Lacey Crawford – Basilio Rodella

Illustrations
Audrey Marcus

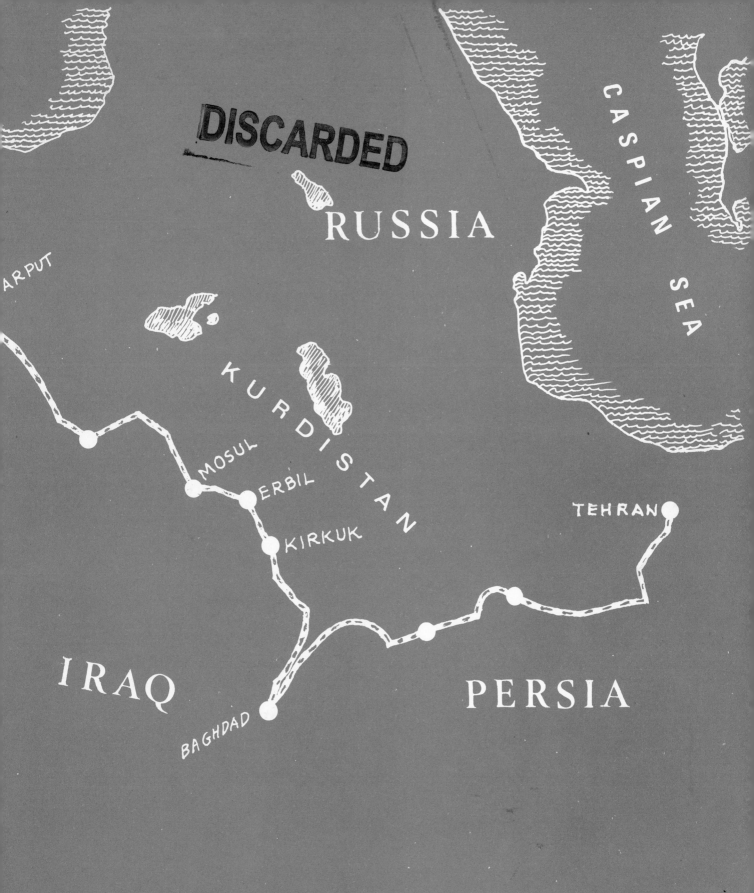

PREFACE

Much has been written about the Holy Land, that small turbulent area in the Middle East linking Asia, Africa and Europe. Throughout the ages it has played a vital role in the ever-unfolding drama of religious history. Jews, Christians, Muslims all revere this land that shelters many of their Holy Places: the Western Wall, the Church of the Holy Sepulchre, al-Aqsa, and others. Its history is well documented in literature, films and countless art forms, to say nothing of the Holy Books – the Old and New Testaments of the Bible, the Quran [Koran] – which record the origins and other events associated with these revealed religions.

Less well known is the fact that four, not three, major revealed religions have close associations with the Holy Land. For over a hundred years – long before the British Mandate and before the Zionist discourses of Herzl – the Bahá'ís were developing ties with 'Akká and Haifa leading to the establishment of their Holy Places, not by deliberate choice of their own, but by reason of the forces of history.

Exiled from his native Persia to Baghdad, Constantinople and Adrianople, Bahá'u'lláh, Founder of the Bahá'í Faith, was brought as a prisoner of the Turkish regime to the Citadel in 'Akká in August 1868 where he remained in confinement for over two years. Though later allowed to reside in other places in and about 'Akká, he remained a political prisoner for the rest of his life. He passed away in 1892 and his remains are entombed in Bahjí, north of 'Akká. His Shrine, regarded by his followers as the holiest spot on earth, is the point toward which the faithful turn their faces daily as they recite their obligatory prayers.

Shoghi Effendi Rabbaní, late Guardian of the Bahá'í Faith, succinctly and authoritatively summarized the teachings of Bahá'u'lláh:

'The Revelation proclaimed by Bahá'u'lláh, His followers believe, is divine in origin, all-embracing in scope, broad in its outlook, scientific in its method, humanitarian in its principles and dynamic in the influence it exerts on the hearts and minds of men. The mission of the Founder of their Faith, they conceive it to be to proclaim that religious truth is not absolute but relative, that Divine Revelation is continuous and progressive, that the Founders of all past religions, though different in the non-essential aspects of their teachings, "abide in the same Tabernacle, soar in the same heaven, are seated upon the same throne, utter the same speech and proclaim the same Faith." His Cause, they have already demonstrated, stands identified with, and revolves around, the principle of the organic unity of mankind as representing the consummation of the whole process of human evolution. This final stage in this stupendous evolution, they assert, is not only necessary but inevitable, that it is gradually approaching, and that nothing short of the celestial potency with which a divinely ordained Message can claim to be endowed can succeed in establishing it.

'The Bahá'í Faith recognizes the unity of God and of His Prophets, upholds the principle of an unfettered search after truth, condemns all forms of superstition and prejudice, teaches that the fundamental purpose of religion is to promote concord and harmony, that it must go hand-in-hand with science, and that it constitutes the sole and ultimate basis of a peaceful, ordered and progressive society. It inculcates the principle of equal opportunity, rights and privileges for both sexes, advocates compulsory education, abolishes extremes of poverty and wealth, exalts work performed in the spirit of service to the rank of worship, recommends the adoption of an auxiliary international language, and provides the necessary agencies for the establishment and safeguarding of a permanent and universal peace.'

The story of the Bahá'ís and the Holy Land is now recounted for the first time in a book designed for general circulation. There will be others as the Faith emerges from relative obscurity. Today there are over four million Bahá'ís in 116,700 localities in 214 independent countries and dependent territories, 148 of which have their own national administrative bodies. The rate of growth and recognition of the Faith is escalating rapidly, particularly because of the attention being focused upon it by the persecution of the Bahá'ís in Iran.

Maintaining close contact with the United Nations since 1947, the Bahá'í International Community presently enjoys consultative status with the United Nations Economic and Social Council (ECOSOC), the United Nations Children's Fund (UNICEF), and association with the United Nations Office of Public Information (OPI) and the United Nations Environment Program (UNEP).

Bahá'í temples are located in Wilmette, Illinois (near Chicago); Kampala, Uganda; Sydney, Australia; Frankfurt, West Germany; Panama City, Panama; Apia, Western Samoa; and New Delhi, India. The New Delhi temple (see page 77) dedicated in December 1986 has attracted world-wide acclaim as one of the architectural marvels of the twentieth century.

The Bahá'í World Center, located in the Haifa-'Akká area, is the hub of this new and dynamic religious community which is now casting the light of Bahá'í teachings into every corner of the planet. Its importance to the progress and development of the family of man and the peace and tranquillity of the nations will be understood and appreciated only gradually as the generality of mankind comes to recognize the station of Bahá'u'lláh.

Haifa
March 1987

HUGH E. CHANCE

CONTENTS

The Shrine of the Báb on Mount Carmel overlooking the City of Haifa

1

HOW BEAUTIFUL
UPON THE MOUNTAINS

*How beautiful upon the mountains are the feet of him
who brings good tidings . . .*

Isaiah 52:7

The morning sun shimmers on the golden dome and turns the white Italian marble to amber. Dark cypress trees point heavenward and sway a little in their upward march along the mountain slopes. Low hedges of dusty green thyme accent the geometry of the gardens that surround the Shrine of the Báb on Mount Carmel in the Holy Land. And always there are the streams of visitors entering the wrought-iron gates that open from the avenue. They walk the pebbled paths to the Shrine, pausing now and then to admire the leaden peacocks, eagles, and graceful urns that mark the way.

'Who are they? Where do they come from?' asks the visitor standing near the entrance to the golden-domed Shrine. He is a young man and he speaks in English with a slight German accent.

The guide, a tall greyhaired lady, smiles. 'They are humanity, they are from everywhere.'

'Are they Bahá'ís?'

'Many are Bahá'ís – they come from all parts of the world. Others are travelers who come with the tours – thousands in a month.'

The young man gazed down the terraced gardens, nine in all, that descend steeply from the Shrine toward the blue Mediterranean and the ships anchored in the harbor of Haifa. Across the bay to the north lies the ancient fortress city of 'Akká, rising out of the sands that rim the shore, white against the distant hills of Lebanon. The air is clear and to the right Mount Hermon lifts a snowy turban to an azure sky, awaiting the Day when David's song will be fulfilled and its very dew will be as a blessing 'for brethren to dwell together in unity'. (Psalms 133:1)

The guide turned to greet a small group of people approaching the Shrine. There was a young black man in African dress, speaking French. One woman wore a blue and gold sari. Others looked European or American. The conversation was animated with the special exhilaration of a family meeting after long separation. An American woman tried to speak in halting French to the young African, then turned to the guide: 'We need that international auxiliary language – *now*!'

The guide accompanied them to the door of the Shrine. The visitors were silent now. They removed their shoes to enter, stepping reverently upon the silken Persian carpets that lined the floor.

The young man stood by, watching quietly. 'Would you like to go inside?' the guide asked.

'I was here yesterday with a tour. I came back alone today – there is something here, a kind of peace.' He hesitated. 'Tell me, if I'm not being too curious – those people – were some of them your family?'

'Family – yes, you could say that! Except that we haven't actually met before. They are Bahá'í pilgrims, from India, America, Ireland, Africa. Bahá'ís are really like a family though, no matter from which part of the world we come. It's the central teaching of our Faith: unity in diversity.'

He was silent, again looking northward over the bay toward 'Akká. She said, 'Every Bahá'í in the world longs to come here – to the Shrine of the Báb and to the Shrine of Bahá'u'lláh near 'Akká. It is our spiritual home.'

Carmel, the mountain of Elijah, the mountain of the Prophets, the mountain of God. Below, rising some two hundred meters from the sea, is the cave of Elijah.

'Who was the Báb?' the young man asked. 'A modern-day Elijah?'

'He was like Elijah – he was a warner. He was like John the Baptist too. He heralded the coming of Bahá'u'lláh, the Founder of the Bahá'í Faith. The Báb is a title. It means "the Gate", one who opens the way.'

She paused. The pilgrims were leaving the Shrine now, some in tears, some with smiles. Turning to her listener again, she said: 'The Báb was much more than a Herald. Bahá'ís believe that he opened a whole new cycle in the spiritual life of all people of the world.'

'Was he a Prophet then?'

'Bahá'ís call both the Báb and Bahá'u'lláh *Manifestations of God*. We believe they are the great Educators of humanity who appear about every thousand years, always when civilization is at a low ebb spiritually and morally, and when materialistic goals dominate.'

'One could say the world today qualifies! Who were these educators?'

'Abraham, Moses, Muhammad, Christ. And less known to the Western world, Krishna, Zoroaster, Buddha. They all taught the same fundamental truths: belief in one God, love of one's neighbor, obedience to the moral and ethical laws the Prophets bring.'

'That's just the trouble,' he said. 'There is no common understanding today as to what constitutes moral and ethical law.'

'This is why a new universal standard is needed, one that can reach the whole world of humanity. The Prophet or Divine Educator renews the Covenant of God in each age and redefines the meaning of the ancient spiritual truths in the light of the needs of the age, so that man can progress.'

'What do you mean by the Covenant of God?' he asked.

'It's God's promise *always* to send His Messenger to guide humanity in its greatest hour of need. Man's part, the purpose of his being, is to recognize the Messenger and obey his teachings. Noah, Abraham, Moses all renewed the Covenant. They are like the links in a continuing chain of Revelation or guidance from God. That is why Jesus said "Before Abraham was, I am." And he connected his teaching with Moses.'

The young man stepped aside as another group entered the Shrine and when the guide was free again, he returned. 'A lot of Christians talk about the second coming of Christ and some expect him to come down from the sky.'

'God's Prophet or Manifestation has always

coming of one who, like a Father, will gather together the scattered peoples of the world, and bring peace . . .'

There was a touch of irony in his voice: 'It's hard to believe today that peace will ever be a lasting thing.'

'I know,' she replied. 'But now is the beginning. The world has been preparing for this for over six thousand years. It is less than a century since Bahá'u'lláh was here. Now there are thousands of Bahá'ís spread across the planet. More important, they come from all tribes, races, nationalities, and from all economic and religious backgrounds. The teachings of Bahá'u'lláh have given them a way to work together, as a great world family.'

The irony was gone now. 'I remember something else I was taught as a child: "The wolf and the lamb shall feed together" – and something about making ploughshares out of swords. But can it ever come? Look at the world . . .'

'It's easy to be discouraged. But sometimes you have to take a broader view of things, a mountain-top view. Since the coming of Bahá'u'lláh, in this last century alone man has conquered space and made the whole world a neighborhood, so to speak. Now we must conquer the nearest space of all, the human heart. That is what the teachings of Bahá'u'lláh can accomplish. They change the hearts and make it possible for Bahá'ís to rise above their old prejudices and barriers and work together in unity. It is really happening!'

A large tour group was approaching. He turned to leave.

'Would you like to read something of the story?' She offered a brochure.

He hesitated. 'I'm not sure what I believe. I think of myself as agnostic. I'm a student of science, I plan to be a physicist.'

been born, lived, and walked the earth like other human beings. But he is chosen and endowed by the Creator to bring the new Message to the people. Jesus often referred to the next appearance as the coming of the Son of man, and said he would come "in the glory [or station] of the Father".'

' "When the Spirit of truth comes, he will guide you into all truth" ', he quoted.

'I see you know your scriptures,' she said. She studied his face a moment. 'Bahá'ís believe that Bahá'u'lláh is the Promised One of all the revealed religions. His coming fulfills the age-old prophecies of all the Holy Books about the

Thousands of pilgrims and tourists visit the Shrine of the Báb each year.

'That's a good place to begin,' she said cordially. 'Bahá'u'lláh teaches that true science and religion are in harmony, like the wings of a bird. The spiritual and material forces complement each other. They have to be in balance, or the result is either superstition or gross materialism, and both are destructive of human progress.'

He nodded, smiling. 'If that could be true it would help a lot of people I know who feel as I do.'

'One has to investigate for oneself,' she said. 'Our teachings admonish everyone to search for truth independently, using both the rational mind and the power of faith.'

He took the brochure. 'You have been very kind and I promise to read it.'

'One more thing,' she said. 'Try to visit Bahjí just outside 'Akká. That is where Bahá'u'lláh lived in his last years after he was released from confinement in the prison-city itself. His Shrine is there. That peace you mention – you will feel it even more strongly – it is like a paradise.'

He looked toward the verdurous expanse stretching up the slopes of Carmel with its ornamental orange trees, flamboyants, bougainvillea, the surrounding palms, and fragrance everywhere. 'I call *this* a paradise.'

Steps on the approach to the Shrine of the Báb

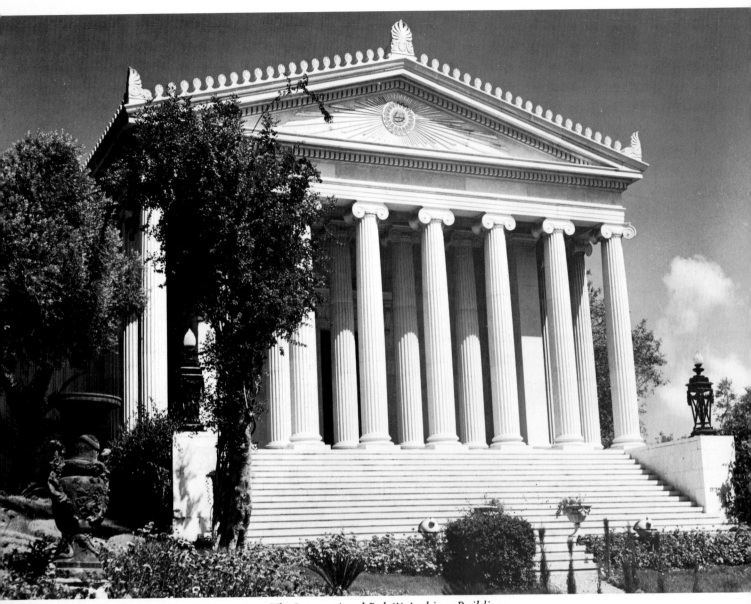

The International Bahá'í Archives Building

2

NEITHER OF THE EAST
NOR OF THE WEST

Passing through the cactus gardens to the main gates of the Shrine of the Báb and across the avenue that cuts through the heart of Carmel, one comes to a wrought-iron gate opening onto a sharply rising path. Close by on the right is a stately marble edifice that is reminiscent of the Parthenon in Athens, though of smaller proportion. It looks very much at home on this craggy mountainside, sheltered by olive, cypress, and eucalyptus trees. It is the International Bahá'í Archives Building and it houses the precious tablets, relics and various documents that memorialize the epic deeds and heroic events that marked the lives of the Central Figures of the Bahá'í Faith and their early followers. Here are reverently preserved the outer material tokens that speak of pain and suffering, of banishment and imprisonment, and of heroic endurance and triumph of a band of exiles from Persia who were led inexorably westward to this shore – even as, millenniums before, the children of Israel were led fatefully eastward into captivity.

High anticipation rules the heart of the pilgrim awaiting the opening of the large bronze doors that lead to the interior of the Archives building. It brings an immediate surprise. At the far end where the afternoon sun penetrates is a large, stained-glass window with exquisite mosaics of blue, amber, and red. It casts a tranquil mauve light upon the rich oriental carpets, the carved ornate cabinets placed throughout the long interior hall, and on the balcony that surrounds three walls.

The relics, inscribed and illuminated tablets, painted miniatures and photographs, all give an immediate poignancy to the lives of the Herald and the Founder of the Bahá'í Faith; to the martyrdom of the youthful Báb in Tabríz in 1850; and to the successive banishments and imprisonments that led Bahá'u'lláh in 1853 from his home in Tehran to the penal colony of 'Akká in 1868. Here are keen reminders that the path of the Prophets is strewn with suffering; their words met with suspicion, with the jeering and violence of the mob, and the jealousy and derision of the powerful and elite.

Aerial view of the Bahá'í gardens on Mount Carmel, Haifa, taken before work began on the Terraces in 1991 (see pp. 101 and 102 below). The Shrine of the Báb appears in the right foreground. Above and to the left are the International Archives Building and the Seat of the Universal House of Justice.

Monument to the memory of Bahíyyih Khánum, eldest daughter of Bahá'u'lláh, founder of the Bahá'í Faith. It is located near the central axis of the arc clearly visible in the photograph above.

Monuments to the memories of the son of Bahá'u'lláh, Mírzá Mihdí, and his mother, Navváb

Here, and in other places, are preserved many of the original letters and writings of the Twin Prophets of the Bahá'í Faith, sealed with their own seals, often penned by their own hands. Thus the words of Bahá'u'lláh in his Tablet of the World:

O people of Justice! Be as brilliant as the light and as splendid as the fire that blazed in the Burning Bush. The brightness of the fire of your love will no doubt fuse and unify the contending peoples and kindreds of the earth . . .

And the words of the Báb, sounding a first call to listening hearts:

I am the Lamp which the Finger of God hath lit within its niche and caused to shine with deathless splendour. I am the Flame of that supernal Light that glowed upon Sinai in the gladsome Spot, and lay concealed in the midst of the Burning Bush.

Not only is the authentic Word itself preserved, signed and sealed – the laws, meditations, prayers, tablets of instruction – but many tokens of everyday life: a comb, seals, a watch, clothing, books – homely, personal things that catch at the heart as one becomes aware that the Revealers of the Word of God, bearing the awesome burden of Prophethood shared by no man, also walked the earth and knew the cares and mortal concerns of all humanity. Time passes unmarked for the pilgrim, brought so close to the earthly life of his Lord, until he once again passes through the heavy portals to the outside world.

Standing outside the Archives building on the portico one gazes out between Ionic pillars at a panorama of landscape and architecture spreading across Carmel in one harmonious prospect.

An awareness comes of a 'master designer' at work – uniquely endowed with artistic perception and extraordinary strength – wresting this thing of beauty from the barren, rocky mountainside. One is not concerned about the ingenuity and prodigious effort needed to resolve problems of retaining walls, of carving out terraces, of establishing water supplies, of securing steel and marble and trees. One revels only in the finished, glorious handiwork.

The effect is formed of individual parts, each unique in itself: the serene memorial gardens, the resting-place of Bahá'u'lláh's own family, secluded by tall cypresses now casting their protective shadows; terraced gardens with radiating paths and star-shaped flower beds; the interspersing of wrought-iron lamps and gates; artistic urns mounted on marble pedestals; leaden peacocks and eagles, symbols of eternal life and victory; and the specially created settings for the stately edifices – the whole unified in one great vista by some magic not easily defined.

A broad pathway cuts an arc across the bosom of Carmel high above the memorial gardens and the International Archives. From its center rises a majestic marble building as if carved out of the very heart of the mountain. It is modern yet reminiscent of the Greek style with its balance and harmony, its grace and solidity, the Corinthian columns and capitals, all made of gleaming white marble from Mount Pentelikon near Athens.

This stately building is the world administrative headquarters of the Bahá'í Faith, the Seat

Views of the newly constructed building for the Seat of the Universal House of Justice

of its supreme governing body, the Universal House of Justice, which was ordained by Bahá'u'lláh himself. Members of more than 130 national and regional administrative bodies of the world, known as National Spiritual Assemblies, gather here quinquennially to cast over 1,000 ballots and elect this supreme institution of the Bahá'í Faith. The nine members who presently serve on this body are drawn from various parts of the world and from several racial and religious backgrounds. From this Seat stream the leadership and guidance for the National Assemblies and for the Bahá'ís in more than 116,000 localities in all continents of the globe. Thus the twin cities of Haifa and 'Akká comprise the spiritual and administrative Center for the entire Bahá'í world.

Looking toward the sea, the Shrine of the Báb again commands the view. Its gleaming dome made of gold-under-glaze tiles rests upon a circular drum which in turn rests upon an octagon that supports eight slender, 'minaret-like spires', all carved in Italy from Chiampo

View looking northwesterly toward the International Archives Building and the Shrine of the Báb

marble. The whole is mounted upon a square arcade with carved Rose Baveno columns and twenty-eight graceful arches, seven on each side. The delicately carved motifs, the green and gold medallions with their special symbology, all serve to embellish this Shrine which is 'neither of the east nor of the west' and which calls 'to mind the glories of the Roman and Islamic schools of architecture combined into one harmonious conception'.[1]

Through the graceful arches of the arcade can be seen an inner wall built of large blocks of native stone. It is part of the original mausoleum raised by 'Abdu'l-Bahá, eldest son of Bahá'u'lláh. That it was built while he was still a prisoner of the Turkish regime was a near miracle and one that almost cost his life. For many years, through two world wars and during the rule of several authorities in the Holy Land, there stood only this one-story structure where the Báb was entombed, awaiting the day when, as promised by 'Abdu'l-Bahá, a lofty edifice of nobler proportion would mark forever the resting-place of the youthful Martyr-Prophet of a world faith.

*   *   *

What does it mean? Why was the body of the Báb brought here from a bloodstained square in far-away Tabríz to rest in the bosom of this holy mountain? What generates the outpouring of love and devotion that brings so many pilgrims here each year to pray and to refresh the fountain of their spirit? Who was the 'master designer' who created these vast gardens of such unique design and serenity? And *who was Bahá'u'lláh,* now entombed near 'Akká, to whom such reverence is given? What forces brought him, once the scion of a noble Persian family, as a prisoner under Turkish decree to this Spot so remote from his native land? *Who are the Bahá'ís* who bear his name, people of such diverse cultural backgrounds who call this land their spiritual home?

Gate in the gardens of the Shrine of Bahá'u'lláh at Bahjí

3

THAT GATES
MAY NOT BE CLOSED

The story begins in Persia, land of ancient dynasties and great kings – kings such as the mighty conqueror Cyrus who encouraged the spread of the monotheistic teaching of Zoroaster; of whom the Lord said, 'He shall fulfill all my purpose . . . Cyrus, whose right hand I have grasped, to subdue nations before him and ungird the loins of Kings, to open doors before him that gates may not be closed.'[2]

Among the nations subdued was Babylonia, enabling Cyrus to release the captive Jews of Babylon and send them back to Jerusalem to rebuild their Temple.

It was the land of Darius, the great administrator, counseled by Daniel, in whose sixth year of reign the Temple was completed so that once again 'the glory of the Lord filled the Lord's house'. Two hundred years would pass before this great Achaemenian dynasty would be brought to a close by young Alexander the Great.

Tradition tells of the wise seers, the Magi, from this region of the world who, three centuries later, studied the Holy Books and the signs in the heavens and set forth to search for another kind of king, born in a humble place of humble parentage in the land of Judea. From this beginning, the words that he spoke were carried around the Mediterranean world so that in time a new civilization spread across the continent of Europe, tumbling the pillars of the mighty Roman Empire that had grown hollow in decline. Powerful institutions came to bear the name of this lowly teacher of the land and seed of Abraham: Jesus the Christ. Towering cathedrals and basilicas that were masterpieces of architecture never before envisioned were raised. One of the most magnificent was the Church of the Divine Wisdom, the Hagia Sophia completed in AD 562 in the city of Constantine, when Byzantium glowed with the brightest splendors of the Christian Dispensation.

A century later in the time of Sassanian decline, a long-lived Persian dynasty* that defeated the Roman Empire, Persia yielded to

* Bahá'u'lláh is a descendant of this dynasty.

the surging vitality of the Arabic followers of Muhammad, a vitality that within a few centuries would spread a bright crescent of Islamic civilization from Spain to India. Nearly a thousand years later when the Islamic sun was setting in Spain, following the fall of Granada and a halting blow at Lepanto, it was still shining in India with the brilliant glow of the Mogul dynasty at Delhi. Its gleam was caught in an exquisite architecture of palaces and mosques, symbolized by the Taj Mahal, a tomb for a lost, loved queen.

During the sixteenth century there arose Islamic Persia's greatest king, Shah Abbas the Great of the Safavid dynasty, who chose Isfahan, sometimes called 'half-the-world', to be his capital. Here along the banks of the Zenda Rud (Zaindeh) he raised a magic city: jeweled mosques with graceful, towering minarets; shrines of delicate tiled domes; fabulous pavilions and palaces, their pillars reflected in pools of water; arched and canopied bridges, perhaps the most artistic bridges the world has seen. One of his structures, the Royal Mosque with its fountains, gardens, pools and flowing Persian script dedicating it to God from Abbas, is considered by many to be one of the world's most beautiful buildings.

It is farther south in the city of Shíráz in Fárs, seat of Persia's beginnings, where Siyyid 'Alí-Muhammad, later known as the Báb, was born on 20 October 1819. According to his teacher, 'Alí-Muhammad showed unusual wisdom and piety even as a very small child. His father died while he was a young lad and from that time he lived with a maternal uncle. At age fifteen he joined his uncle in his trade as a merchant, spending much time at the Persian Gulf port of Bushire. Some few years later he was given management of the business and became widely known among clients and fellow-tradesmen for a scrupulous honesty and fairness in the conduct of his business affairs.

Sometimes during these years the Báb traveled the dusty roads from Bushire to Shíráz in the trembling heat that blended together the lavender-grey mountains and pale skies. In his twenty-second year he journeyed to the holy cities of Iraq and spent some months in Karbala where he visited the Shrine of his own illustrious ancestor, the Imam Husayn, grandson of the Prophet Muhammad. Here he made contact with the famed teacher, Siyyid Kázim, who had taken on the work of his predecessor, Shaykh Ahmad, proclaiming that the hour was swiftly approaching when the Promised One of God, the Qá'im, would appear.

Shíráz has been called the city of saints and poets, of nightingales and roses, and among its beauty spots are the shrines erected for the poets Hafiz and Saadi. Once for a few years, under the Zend dynasty, Shíráz knew brief glory as the ruling city of Persia. Once it gave its name to a school of Persian painting, an art that recorded with jewel-like perfection the deeds of historic and legendary figures: Khosrau the Great and his beautiful wife Shirin; Majnun and Laila, the oriental Romeo and Juliet; the brave hero

The Koran Gate, northern entrance to the city of Shíráz, Iran

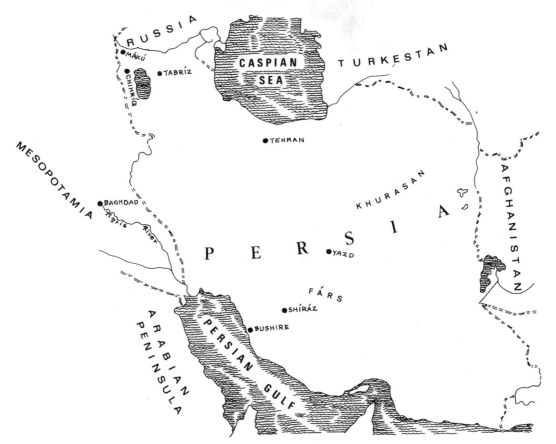

Persia in the Nineteenth Century

Rustam, and Iskandar (Alexander the Great) who, though having been their conqueror, was esteemed by many Persians for his magnanimity to the conquered Queen Mother and for his deep love of Persian culture; of interiors with richly colored tiles and carpets, and elegantly furbished tents; and of fabled birds and beasts all poised as if for eternity against a fairyland landscape of flowers and tamarisk trees.

In this ancient land, now in the time of the Báb misruled, priest-ridden and burdened with a royal bureaucracy, and in this city of Shíráz, Siyyid 'Alí-Muḥammad declared his Mission to the learned young Mullá Ḥusayn from the province of Khurasan to the north, whom he designated the first to accept his claim as the Bearer of a new Revelation from God. This historic proclamation began at sunset in a small upper room in the house of the Báb and lasted into the hours of dawn. In much less than a century, this eve of 23 May 1844 was to become a Holy Day of major observance for the Bahá'ís throughout the world.

Mullá Ḥusayn was an accomplished scholar. He was also an earnest seeker, one of that select number who had gathered in Karbala under the guidance of Siyyid Káẓim, whose final admonishment before his passing in 1843 was for his followers to remain pure-hearted and alert for the coming of the 'Lord of the Age', he whom the whole world awaited as Redeemer.

Although in his heart Mullá Ḥusayn was ardently searching for such a fulfillment, he did not anticipate that it would begin at the Kaziran Gate of Shíráz as he was entering the city dusty and travel-worn from the city of Bushire. Here beneath spreading, broad-leaved plane trees he was greeted for the first time by the Báb with such kindliness and courtesy, and with such an irresistible appeal and attraction that he was overwhelmingly drawn to listen.

History records the effect that the Báb's words, soon to be spoken in that upper room, had upon Mullá Ḥusayn: 'Excitement, joy, awe, and wonder stirred the depths of my soul,' he said. 'I felt possessed of such courage and power . . . The universe seemed but a handful of dust in my grasp.'

Room in the House of the Báb in Shíráz where he declared his mission to Mullá Ḥusayn. The House was completely destroyed by fanatical mobs in 1979–80 during the persecutions of the Bahá'ís in Iran.

4

A SUNBURST AT MIDNIGHT

For Mullá Ḥusayn and for the other 'Letters of the Living' as the Báb's first disciples were called, the world would indeed become a 'handful of dust' in the course of a few tumultuous years. They were years that stirred the people of Persia and surrounding lands with the new Message. In a few speeding decades it would lead with history's own prescience to the 'heart of the world', the Holy Land on the eastern Mediterranean shore.

The Báb was twenty-five years of age. He had only six years in which to proclaim his prophetic mission before his life would end before a firing squad in the noontide heat of a summer day in the public square of Tabríz. His Message was a call to a New Day – a universal day – one that would touch the lives of all who dwelt on earth and in the course of time usher in that age of peace and brotherhood foretold in all the Holy Books of the past. He well knew that his teachings would be harshly repulsed and would draw virulent antagonism from many of the powerful and elite. He foretold his own martyrdom and that of many of those who chose to follow him.

Above all, the Báb taught his followers to look for another, the Promised One of all ages, who would shortly appear with a Revelation greater than his own, with laws for a universal civilization. He himself was the Báb, *the Gate*, or Door – a Herald sent to prepare the way. His coming marked both the end of millenniums of prophecy and expectancy, and the dawn of that age of peace proclaimed by all the Prophets of old.

Impelled intuitively to Shíráz in their course of search, the Letters of the Living independently found and recognized the Báb. One of these, a remarkable poetess, Táhirih, did not meet him in person. His disciples were, the Báb said in a farewell address to them in Shíráz as he sent them on their way, 'the bearers of the Name of God' for the New Day. 'Ponder the words of Jesus addressed to His disciples,' he admonished them: 'Let your light shine before the eyes of men.'[4] It was their task to awaken the people to the Hour in which they lived, even as the

Its lights are strong; . . . more intense because they seem like a sunburst at midnight.[3]

disciples of Christ had been bidden to 'go into all the world and preach the gospel . . .'

So they went forth in eagerness with the new truth they had embraced, carrying it like a flame throughout their land and beyond, lighting wherever they went the fires of an undying faith in the promises of God – lighting as well fires of antagonism that flared in hearts and minds too constricted to understand the past or see the glory of the future. The spirit that embraced the new believers, the Báb told them, was the same as that of old – the power that had assisted Abraham, Moses, Jesus, and Muhammad in their days.

Almost from the beginning of his Mission, the Báb was a captive, passed from one authority, religious or civil, to another. The road led northward to a remote mountain region near the Russian and Turkish frontiers. Here in bleak fortresses, he was closely confined for the last three years of his life.

As he journeyed north, in custody, visitors came from far and near to listen to his words, to ask questions, to ponder the meaning of his Message. And even as truth, like the sun, brings out the hidden recesses, so was the response evoked by the Báb. Many of his guards and captors, ordered to maintain severe restrictions on their captive, found themselves being irresistibly attracted to him. They could not withstand the love and kindness the Báb extended to them, the power of the words he spoke, and the calm nobility with which he conducted himself as their prisoner. Others, including those who sat in judgment on him at a mock trial, were unmoved. They feared the extraordinary attraction that caused people to throng to the Báb, and they were incapable of comprehending the true meaning of his teaching. They saw in it only a threat to their position as religious or political leaders, and they com-

Site of the fortress of <u>Chihríq</u> where the Báb was imprisoned during the two years before his martyrdom in 1850

mitted themselves to silencing this youth once and forever. And the mobs were swayed this way and that, moved as mobs are, neither by love nor reason but by a fanaticism that cheers one day and calls for blood the next.

Ten thousand crowded the barracks square and surrounding rooftops on that July noon when they brought forth the Báb and a youthful companion for execution. The colonel of an Armenian regiment was assigned to carry out the order. As the hour drew near he grew increasingly distraught for in his heart he felt the innocence of the Báb.

'Enable me to free myself from the obligation to shed your blood,' he pleaded with the Báb.

The Báb spoke gently. 'Follow your instructions, and if your intention be sincere, the Almighty is surely able to relieve you . . .'

The regiment, 750 strong and ranged in three

26

files, took its position. Then volley after volley was poured forth at the prisoners now bound against the wall. The crowd gasped – only the ropes that held them had been rent and the Báb had left the scene, to complete an interrupted conversation with one of his followers who served as his amanuensis.

The Colonel, much shaken, ordered his entire regiment to leave the square and he refused any further involvement. Another colonel volunteered for the odious task and once again the prisoner was led forth and bound, with his young companion. Just before they killed him the Báb looked calmly out at the mobs before him and said: 'The day will come when you will have recognized Me; that day I shall have ceased to be with you.'

Many of those who believed in the Báb had already given their lives – and there were many more to follow. Among those who heard and believed, much to the agitation of their peers, were a number of religious scholars and learned ones in the law and religious jurisprudence. And like Mullá Ḥusayn, the first believer, they gave up their titles and a life of worldly ease and honor, often exchanging them for a martyr's death. Some few were courtiers and members of the nobility. But the majority were people of trade and business, artisans, government clerks, scribes, bookbinders, carpenters, poets, peasants, and shepherds.

It was a young shepherd boy from the province of Khurasan, known as Nabíl, who nourished a gifted pen that would one day chronicle the deeds and events surrounding the life of the Báb, and of the one he preceded and foretold – Bahá'u'lláh. In one of history's omniscient footnotes, this shepherd boy, awakened to the call of the Báb in his youth, was to witness for half a century the dramatic episodes that marked the advent of a new and universal Revelation. In his eloquent eyewitness account, called *The Dawn-Breakers*, painstakingly documented, one learns intimately of the tribulations and triumphs that swirled around the central figures of this spiritual drama like a 'sunburst at midnight'.

A Persian Joan of Arc

Unique among these figures was a lone woman – peerless in her courage, tragic, yet triumphant withal. Sarah Bernhardt longed to portray her on the stage. In Europe she was called the 'Persian Joan of Arc' and like Joan she was martyred while still young. Her fame swept across the horizons of Persia and to the West before she fell, like a meteor, still blazing. But it was not for the cause of battle or a single nation that she gave her life, but the cause of universal peace, and particularly the cause of freedom for women. Without doubt she was the world's first woman suffrage martyr.

Facing death, she declared to her captors: 'You can kill me as soon as you like, but you cannot stop the emancipation of women!'

Ṭáhirih (the Pure One), as she came to be known among her religious compatriots, possessed beauty, brilliance, and a magnetic charm that greatly attracted people to her. She came from a wealthy, highly respected family, the father holding a high ecclesiastical position. But it was her gift as an accomplished poetess and especially as a scholar that made her a rare phenomenon among women in that day and place. So well versed was she that many of the learned doctors of religious law held discourses with her and were astonished at the depth of her thought. Frequently her ideas did not fit in with their age-old traditional views, accumulated through centuries, and now crystallized and encrusted with countless man-made theories, and so they arose to silence her.

A Persian lady of the nineteenth century

Ecbatana of the Medes, captured by Cyrus the Great twenty-three centuries before. Nearby, tradition says, are the tombs of Queen Esther and Mordecai. Her road led near the Behistun monument near Kermanshah where Darius I had his deeds inscribed in stone in three ancient languages – sometimes called the Rosetta Stone of Asia.

Doubtless the thoughts of Ṭáhirih, this dauntless woman born out of her time, were not on tokens of the past as she traveled by howdah the five hundred dusty miles, accompanied by a younger sister and other companions. The breezes of the New Day had stirred her spirit and enkindled her mind with an eager expectancy.

A sharp disappointment awaited Ṭáhirih in Karbala. Siyyid Káẓim had died shortly before her arrival. But here she met many of his students and here she soon became a confirmed follower of the Báb. Quickly she tasted of the persecution and harassment that would bring her a martyr's death in less than a decade. For she would not be silenced. She taught her new Faith openly, eloquently, even though she knew the price that such audacity would ultimately demand. One of her poems reads:

At the gates of my heart there tramp the feet and camp the hosts of calamity. . .[5]

It was a prescient inspiration. She returned to her home in Qazvín. She taught the Cause of the Báb fearlessly there and in other cities. Many were confirmed. Countless others were deeply moved by the cogency of her argument and the eloquence of her words but lacked the temerity needed for commitment. She was a constant stimulus to her fellow believers, quickening them into bolder action in spreading the new message. Once at such a time she appeared among a group of them – all men – without her veil, in order to emphasize the laws of the New

Count Gobineau, a French diplomat who was one of the first Europeans to write about the new religion, said: 'Many people who knew her and heard her at different periods of her life have invariably told me . . . that when she spoke one felt stirred to the depths of one's soul . . .'

Ṭáhirih was the only woman disciple of the Báb, one of the Letters of the Living who, not long after his meeting with Mullá Ḥusayn in the upper room in Shíráz, had discovered him through their own abounding faith and zealous search. Ṭáhirih too had studied the writings of the famed teacher, Siyyid Káẓim, who had prepared Mullá Ḥusayn and many others for the New Day. She corresponded with him and became eager to meet him in person.

From her home in Qazvín not far from the Elburz mountains that rim the south Caspian shore, Ṭáhirih undertook an overland journey to meet Siyyid Káẓim in Karbala, near Baghdad. The road led through Hamadan, the ancient

Dispensation and the new station of women. It was an event so shocking in that day and place as to cause some to desert their new Faith entirely.

The 'hosts of calamity' gathered around her increasingly and often she was held in confinement as powerful religious leaders feared and opposed her influence. More than once Bahá'u'lláh came to her rescue: for he had from the beginning championed the Cause of the Báb and had arisen fearlessly to protect and assist the believers as the winds of persecution swept around them, bringing often the sting of death.

Now in the summer of 1852, just two years after the Báb had been martyred in Tabríz, a city made known to the West by the visit of Marco Polo more than five centuries before, Bahá'u'lláh was himself confined in the Black Pit in Tehran. Daily some of the followers of the new religion confined with him were taken out and brutally killed.

Ṭáhirih was put to death in Tehran in August of that year. Her enemies believed that her voice was silenced now forever. But the flame of her life and her death became instead a blazing star to light up that midnight sky long after her enemies and their generation had passed. Today among many tribes and nations, and in a myriad of tongues, Ṭáhirih is remembered and loved and her story retold. And in these lands numbers of little girls have been made her namesakes and proudly carry the name of Ṭáhirih. But the modern world that embraces freedom and equality for women has yet to claim its own.

'The appearance of such a woman,' Professor Edward G. Browne, famed orientalist of Cambridge, has written, 'is in any country and any age a rare phenomenon, but in such a country as Persia it is a prodigy – nay, almost a miracle.'[6]

* * *

How much did they understand, those first valiant believers? So many willingly, even joyfully, gave their lives in the path of the Báb. Did they fully comprehend the universality of his teachings – that thousands of years and many dispensations of the past had reached their culmination in the Message they had embraced? What they did know was that the one they had sought had been found, that his words were true, and that they were the first springs that had welled out from his Revelation. *The dawn had come and they were the first streaks of light on the horizon.*

The seeming tragedy of their brief lives and the violence and brutality so often directed against them by the bedimmed leadership of their day must be measured against the beauty of the Message they bore – a Message of hope and love for 'all the peoples and nations of both East and West'.

The Mansion at Bahjí, built in 1868–70. It was secured as a residence for Bahá'u'lláh in 1879 when it was abandoned by its owner during an epidemic.

Ornamental gate on the pathway to the Shrine of Bahá'u'lláh

5

BLESSED IS THE SPOT

A passage in the writings of Bahá'u'lláh, much loved by Bahá'ís and others who are familiar with it, reads:

Blessed is the spot, and the house, and the place,
and the city, and the heart, and the mountain,
and the refuge, and the cave, and the valley,
and the land, and the sea, and the island,
and the meadow where mention of God hath been made,
and His praise glorified.

No spot or house or place on earth is so sacred and beloved to Bahá'ís as is the Shrine of Bahá'u'lláh with its adjacent Mansion. Situated in a 'meadow' near the sea and the city of 'Akká – the ancient fortress-city that rises tier upon tier of civilizations past – it stands serene in the midst of exquisite gardens. The verse quoted above, now set to music and recorded by a world-renowned opera baritone, seems uniquely to apply to this Shrine, and to its sister Shrine of the Báb across the bay on Mount Carmel.[7] Both are visited annually by thousands of people from many lands, Bahá'í pilgrims and others.

It is the cherished hope of every Bahá'í in the world to visit these holy places at least once in a lifetime, though there are many who come again and again. Arriving first at Mount Carmel, the Bahá'í pilgrim pays homage at the resting-place of the Báb, the Herald of his Faith. Sacred and moving as is this experience, the summit of the pilgrim's visit to the Holy Land is the Shrine of Bahá'u'lláh. Later there are visits to many places, in the environs of Haifa and 'Akká particularly, made historically significant to Bahá'ís since the inception of their Faith in the Holy Land in 1868. Bahá'ís also visit and revere the many places sacred to the memory of the Founders of Judaism, Christianity, and Islam, where the 'mention of God hath been made, and His praise glorified'. Whether or not the religion of their forefathers was rooted in the soil of this land, their belief in the Holy Books of the past and in the continuity of Revelation is a fundamental spiritual heritage given to them by Bahá'u'lláh.

Entrance to the Shrine of Bahá'u'lláh

Here on the broad plains of 'Akká, surrounded by farms and groves of citrus and olive, is the last house occupied by Bahá'u'lláh during his twenty-four-year sojourn in Palestine as a prisoner of the Turkish government. It is called Bahjí, 'place of delight'. Over the entrance of this Mansion, as it is called, engraved on a marble plaque, is this Arabic inscription, placed there in the year 1870 by its builder and owner:

> Greetings and salutations rest upon this Mansion, which increaseth in splendour through the passage of time.
> Manifold wonders and marvels are found therein, and pens are baffled in attempting to describe them.

Among the 'wonders', of which the builder could have had no foreknowledge, was the path of events that brought Bahá'u'lláh – then confined to a dismal cell in the Citadel of 'Akká – from that walled prison city to this tranquil spot in the country, here to spend the remaining twelve years of his life. He is buried nearby in a simple, one-story building that has not yet received the magnificent embellishment destined for it. It is the supreme place of pilgrimage for Bahá'ís.

Eighteen years before Bahá'u'lláh's arrival in 'Akká, the life of the youthful Báb had been expended that the way might be prepared for the Mission of Bahá'u'lláh. That Mission Bahá'u'lláh had succinctly expressed in words recorded by Professor E. G. Browne of Cambridge, who had sought an interview and been received by him in this very Mansion in 1890, not long before his passing on 29 May 1892:

> . . . That all nations should become one in faith and all men as brothers; that the bonds of affection and unity between the sons of men should be strengthened; that diversity of religion should cease, and differences of race be annulled . . . so it shall be; these fruitless strifes, these ruinous wars shall pass away, and the 'Most Great Peace' shall come . . . Is not this that which Christ foretold?[8]

To have a perfect orientation to Bahjí with its extensive gardens one should ideally view it first from the air. From such a vantage point can be seen the wide tree-lined path circling the main area around the Shrine and the Mansion. Radiating from the circle like sunrays are many pebbled paths, tawny in hue, that converge upon the central edifices, forming large quadrants. Two of the gardens thus shaped are separated by a series of large rectangular gardens. One of these is comprised of three terraces that rise like the steps of a Mayan pyramid, intersected by steps and iron gates and walkways that run the full length. In addition to the aesthetic appeal of this terraced garden with its cypresses and red geraniums – one writer has likened it to the Biblical gardens of Babylon – it forms a magnificent viewing platform for the surrounding expanse. All of the gardens are

Aerial view of the gardens at Bahjí

Detail of urn in the gardens at Bahjí

adorned with star-shaped flower-beds, marble and leaden urns, and other ornaments strikingly posed against carpets of green grass.

The visitor approaches the Shrine of Bahá'u'-lláh from the north, beginning at a point not far from a highway that still marks the ancient coastal road to Tyre. He walks a long path bordered by flowering trees and shrubs. Passing through a beautiful wrought-iron gate of magnificent proportion, the way leads directly to the entrance of the Shrine, over smooth pebbles from the shores of the Sea of Galilee that would have been familiar to the feet of Jesus. A myriad aspects of beauty enchant the eye along the way. To the left rises the triple-terraced garden, ablaze with a sea of red blossoms. To the right one of the quadrants focuses its rays upon the Shrine. Close to the Shrine stands the Mansion of Bahjí, majestic in mien, a large square two-storied structure of arched balconies above and colonnades below. Bougainvillea and jacaranda bloom profusely. Nearby are ancient pine trees that once sheltered Bahá'u'lláh, seemingly oblivious of any mortality.

If the visitor is a Bahá'í pilgrim his immediate destination is the Shrine of Bahá'u'lláh. He passes through a small iron gate and an outer court. Reverently he removes his shoes before passing through the large oaken doors, carved in Tuscany, reminiscent of the portals to the Bahá'í Archives on Mount Carmel. The glassed-in upper story of the inner court sheds a stream of sunlight upon a small island garden in the center, and upon the richly blended hues of Oriental carpets that cover the surrounding passageway.

Farther on is the threshold of the room beneath whose floor the remains of Bahá'u'lláh were laid to rest. There are fresh flowers at the threshold, reminding the pilgrim how much he loved flowers and all growing things, and how

The hoopoe

when they were brought to him, he lovingly distributed them among his guests. In this sanctuary are placed beautiful porphyry urns, Chinese *cloisonné* vases and other exquisite art objects – these and the many Oriental carpets the gifts of Bahá'ís of East and West.

It is the pilgrim's supreme bounty to approach that threshold – there to express his heart's gratitude and praise, to offer his prayers, his pleas for strength and illumination to serve out his life in the path of that 'Most Great Peace' his Lord has designed for the world of humanity. It is his point of adoration, as the wall of Solomon's Temple in Jerusalem is for Jews, St. Peter's in Rome for Roman Catholics, and the Black Stone in Mecca for Muslims.

Close by in the Mansion is the upper room of Bahá'u'lláh where pilgrims enter to pray and meditate and where he was visited by Professor Browne. Of that visit, Browne wrote:

The face of him on whom I gazed I can never forget, though I cannot describe it. Those piercing eyes seemed to read one's very soul; power and authority sat on that ample brow . . .[8]

The visitor is free to roam through the gardens, to inhale the fragrance of jasmine and orange blossoms and other sweet-scented flowers and shrubs. Palm doves warble in the trees, their 'conversation' singularly appropriate to the peaceful atmosphere. A large-crested hoopoe flashes his black and white feathers among the vines. A symbol of endurance, like the olive tree and the thorn, he lays claim to the long memories of this land, to the days of Moses and before, as he goes about his curious ways.

The spirit does not weary here. It is as if all the senses have reached their highest level at the threshold of beauty itself and have found a meeting place with the intangible longing of the soul.

'In its radius,' writes an eminent scholar and historian of the Bahá'í Faith about Bahjí, 'one can experience that peace for which one's soul has ever yearned.'[9]

The ancient pines at Bahjí

Another view of the Mansion at Bahjí (left). Here Bahá'u'lláh passed away on 29 May 1892 and was laid to rest in the building on the right.

View of the balcony of the Mansion at Bahjí looking toward the room occupied by Bahá'u'lláh

Gardens in the olive grove at Bahjí

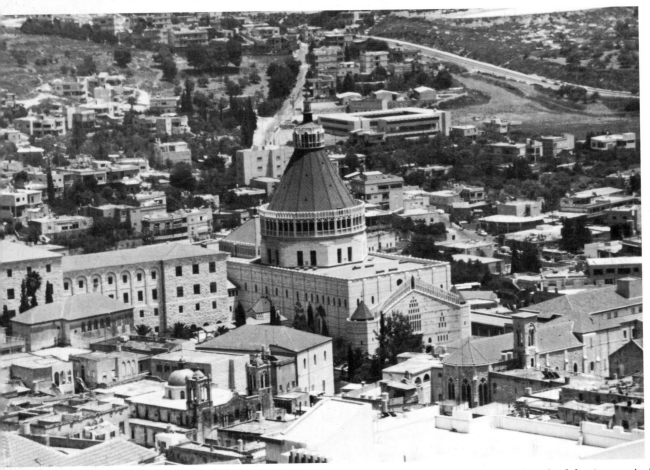

The Church of the Annunciation at Nazareth, near the spot where tradition says Joseph maintained his carpenter shop

Saint Peter's Church at Tabgha on the Sea of Galilee, near the site associated with the story of the multiplication of loaves and fishes, looking toward Tiberias in the distance

THE NEST OF THE PROPHETS

The Holy Land is referred to by Shoghi Effendi, Guardian of the Bahá'í Faith, as 'the Land promised by God to Abraham, sanctified by the Revelation of Moses, honored by the lives and labors of the Hebrew patriarchs, judges, kings and prophets, revered as the cradle of Christianity, and as the place where Zoroaster. . . "held converse with some of the Prophets of Israel", and associated by Islam with the Apostle's night-journey, through the seven heavens, to the throne of the Almighty.' (*God Passes By*, p. 183)

The Dome of the Rock (Mosque of Omar) on the Temple Mount in Jerusalem, said to have been built over the place where Abraham offered his son as a sacrifice.

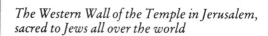

The Western Wall of the Temple in Jerusalem, sacred to Jews all over the world

39

The sea gate at ʿAkká

6

THE WILDERNESS
AND THE
SOLITARY PLACE

It was afternoon of a sultry August day in 1868 when the crowd gathered at the harbor in 'Akká, staring at the Persian prisoners arriving on their shores. The sailing vessel from Haifa was filled with nearly seventy passengers, half of them women and children. The crowd beside the sea gate looked on with curiosity. Some mocked and shouted insults, for already prejudice and calumny had done their work. Their sea journey had begun at Gallipoli on the Turkish Sea of Marmara, and they were being banished to the penal colony at 'Akká. It would be the fourth and last exile for Bahá'u'lláh, his family and companions, and it was not expected that they would long survive the harsh conditions to be imposed upon them.

It had taken sixteen years for the chain of events to unfold that brought Bahá'u'lláh from the subterranean dungeon of the Síyáh-Chál (the Black Pit) of Tehran, where he was imprisoned in August of 1852, to a prison cell in 'Akká in August of 1868. He was fifty-one years of age. Nearly half those years had now been spent in service to the Cause of the Báb and to his own Cause, for the burden of the martyred Prophet's Mission had, as the Báb foretold, fallen upon his shoulders.

The summons had come clearly to him as he lay in that loathsome pit, devoid of all light, with heavy chains cutting into the flesh, and with his companions and fellow disciples of the Báb, as they were then known, taken out daily to meet death. Like the voice that spoke to Moses, to Muhammad, to Jesus, and other Prophets of old, it could not be ignored. Even before the Báb's martyrdom in Tabríz and during the long captivity preceding it, it was Bahá'u'lláh who had fearlessly stepped into the maelstrom of persecution and violence to assist and protect the increasingly beleaguered band of the Báb's followers. One of his first acts following the Báb's death had been to devise a way to rescue his remains that had been cast by a moat outside the city. One of his last acts some forty years later would be to pitch his tent on Mount Carmel and indicate to his beloved eldest son, 'Abdu'l-Bahá, the spot on that mountain where the Báb's remains would find their final resting-place, and where a beautiful sanctuary would be erected to his memory.

Bahá'u'lláh was of noble birth. He was born Ḥusayn-'Alí in a family of wealth and position, his father once a Minister of State. He was expected to follow family tradition, to accept the titles, honors, and position that were his by right of birth. But he chose to follow an inner light – one that led to prison and lifelong exile while he labored to reveal his Message of great hope for the world. It was during the early years of his ministry that Ḥusayn-'Alí became known as Bahá'u'lláh (the Glory of God).

As a young boy, Bahá'u'lláh loved to explore the countryside, to frequent wooded mountains and streams and enjoy the companionship of wild creatures that dwelt there. Rather than seeking position at court, he showed concern for the poor and dispirited and sought ways to alleviate their burdens. While still a lad of only thirteen or fourteen he became known in his father's circles for his learning. Scholars and doctors of religious learning listened with astonishment and respect to his comments on deep philosophic and religious questions. He was only twenty-two years of age when his father died and he assumed responsibility for the family as eldest son. He was urged to accept a court function, but a Minister of the court said: 'Leave him to himself. . . . He has some higher aim in view. . . . His thoughts are not like ours. Let him alone.'

After the death of the Báb it was felt by the authorities that they had been successful in stamping out the new religion claiming allegiance throughout the land. Then an event occurred that was to unleash an even greater holocaust. A deranged youth, claiming allegiance to the Báb but not comprehending his true Mission, made a futile attack upon the life of the Shah. The youth was instantly killed but now there arose a new clamor for vengeance against all the Báb's followers. Instead of seeking escape, Bahá'u'lláh rode into the center of the storm to face the authorities, to advise them of the truth of the Cause, to offer logical explanations. But logic and truth were not in demand by his enemies. He was cast into the Black Pit in darkness and in chains. His beautiful home was seized and pillaged. Almost every day he saw some of his companions taken out of the Pit and put to death. Four months later, miraculously alive but broken in health, Bahá'u'lláh was released from the Black Pit to begin the series of exiles that would claim the remainder of his life; and which, as with Abraham of old, would propel him westward, beyond his own designs, finally to the land once called Canaan.

Immediately after release from prison, his health still precarious, Bahá'u'lláh, with his family and a few companions, made a forced journey under military escort to Baghdad caused by reason of an edict of the Shah expelling him from his native land. They were ill-prepared for the journey. It was January. They suffered severely from lack of clothing and protection from the cold of the snow-covered passes of the Zagros mountains.

His eldest son, 'Abdu'l-Bahá, eight years of age, and his little daughter Bahíyyih, a child of six, would, with their mother, remember forever the terror-stricken days in Tehran and the cold mountain journey. Yet, in spite of those memories, the hardships they had suffered, and the uncertainty of the days ahead, they sensed in Bahá'u'lláh on his release a new joy, a power of assurance, that seemed to radiate from him.

'[It seemed] to enfold him like a shining vesture,' his daughter recalled many years later. 'At that time we were only aware of the wonder

The bridge across the Tigris at Baghdad

of it, without understanding . . .'

Not long after, 'Abdu'l-Bahá, at that young age, recognized his father's true station. He *knew* his father was the one foretold by the Báb! Through all the tortuous years ahead, it was this eldest son who became his father's greatest shield and helper. Who could foretell that this small lad, whose entire life would be hazardously lived in exile and prison, would one day be held in high esteem by many of the great and renowned of the West who would seek his presence in the capitals of Europe and America? That one day a noted president of a great American university would invite him to speak, saying, ' 'Abdu'l-Bahá will surely unite the East and the West, for He walks the mystical way with practical feet.'[10]

One by one, the scattered followers of the Báb, hunted, leaderless and forlorn, found their way to Bahá'u'lláh in Baghdad. His house thronged with visitors of all kinds: scholars, nobility, government officials, men of business, and always the less fortunate ones in life who sought his aid. Some came to pose abstruse religious questions and philosophical problems. Others came to argue, to denounce, and often left humbly, their vision enlarged and their spiritual insight broadened. Some religious authorities, moved by jealousy or fear, joined in intrigue with the Persian court in efforts to bring about his downfall. Plans were made to take his life. But he continued to walk among them, fearless and unharmed.

Once, in the midst of confusion brought on by the claims of an envious half-brother, who was zealous for his own leadership, Bahá'u'lláh went away to the mountains of Kurdistan for a solitary sojourn in the wilderness – even as Moses and Christ and Muhammad. Like Elijah, he lived for a time in caves. After many months he returned to a bereft community that eagerly welcomed him back. Soon his home was once again a center of hospitality and light. Some of his greatest works began to flow from his pen: *Hidden Words, The Book of Certitude, The Seven Valleys,* and *The Four Valleys,* and a host of illuminating tablets and dissertations, often written to individuals to answer their questions – all forming part of a vast, future storehouse of Bahá'í scripture.

Could he be the one foretold by the Báb? Many wondered. Some felt it intuitively. They rallied under his leadership; but still, he did not openly declare his Mission or reveal his true purpose.

They had not long to wait. The first decade of exile was drawing to a close. With it came a summons from the Sultan of Turkey, urged on by the Persian court, for Bahá'u'lláh to proceed

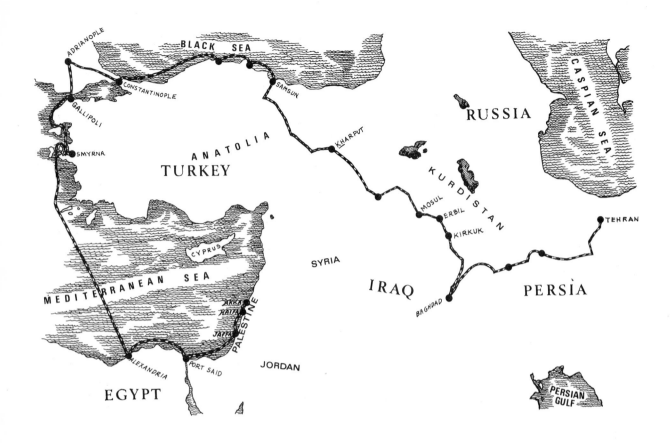

Route of Bahá'u'lláh's exile from his home in Tehran to Iraq, Turkey, and the Holy Land

to Constantinople (Istanbul), seat of the Otto-man Empire, then in decline but still spreading its rule over much of the Middle East and into Europe.

In preparing for the long journey by land and sea, Bahá'u'lláh pitched his tent in a garden across the Tigris River, now known to Bahá'ís as the Garden of Riḍván (Paradise). Here, in a setting luxuriant with roses brought by his companions, he dwelt for twelve days. Here he proclaimed his Mission: he *was* the one foretold by the Báb and promised by the Prophets of old in all the Holy Books.

At that moment, halfway round the world, the American nation, new and yet unmelded, was convulsed in civil war. Even as the believers assembled in the Riḍván Garden, a leading general of that Western Republic prepared for a great and decisive battle – the siege of Vicks-burg – in a war that would shatter the bonds of

slavery. It would be the first nation of the West whose people would respond some few decades hence to the new Call from the East.

On that April day in 1863 there was great rejoicing in the Riḍván Garden. There was sadness too for there were many destined to remain behind, no longer within the radius of Bahá'u'lláh's loving counsel. As he left Baghdad for the last time, huge crowds gathered – men, women, children, of all ages and all walks of life, often with tears streaming down their faces. The Governor of Baghdad who had frequently paid tribute to the character and wisdom of Bahá'u'-lláh, came to bid him a reluctant farewell and to offer assistance. Many even who had conspired to have him expelled, regretted it now at the end.

'Formerly they insisted upon your departure,' the Governor said. 'Now, however, they are even more insistent that you should remain.'

But the die was cast. A few weeks earlier

Bahá'u'lláh had foretold that a new stage of exile was looming on the horizon. Only he could foresee that this twelve-day period in the Riḍván Garden, wherein he had revealed his Mission to a few chosen ones, would be observed in years to come throughout the whole world as the most important festival of the Bahá'í year.

Preparation for the long journey was an immense task. Horses were obtained; howdahs, tents, and other supplies were mounted on mules. A beautiful roan stallion was obtained for Bahá'u'lláh and for the first time many witnessed his superb horsemanship. Previously on his excursions in and about the city he had either walked or chosen to ride a donkey. 'Abdu'l-Bahá, now nineteen years old, assumed heavy responsibilities along the way, securing camp sites, procuring food, attending to the needs of the company, often going without sleep for long periods.

The caravan proceeded through valley and mountain pass, across swift rivers, often as many as thirty miles a day, traveling frequently in the cool of the night. Sometimes Bahá'u'lláh halted the caravan in order that all might look upon a sublime view of nature and be both spiritually and physically refreshed.

Their route took them near many ancient historical sites: the traditional site of the fiery furnace recorded in the Book of Daniel, near Kirkuk, now an oil field and refinery; Arbela (Erbil), not far from the place where the last of the Achaemenian kings was decisively defeated by Alexander the Great in 331 BC. Farther on, east of the Tigris, were the ruins of Nineveh, the great capital of Assyria where Jonah had gone reluctantly at the bidding of the Lord to 'cry against' the transgressions of the people. Across the river to the west rose the minarets and domes of Mosul, a picturesque city where the caravan halted for several days. All along the way Bahá'u'lláh was treated with respect by governors and people and shown considerable hospitality. After Mosul the caravan headed northwest up into the forested mountains of Anatolia. By the time they reached Samsun, the Turkish port on the Black Sea, almost four months had passed.

The howdah, a means of travel in the mid-nineteenth century

Hagia Sophia, Constantinople

7

TO THE CITY
OF GOD'S COMMAND

After some days Bahá'u'lláh and his company boarded a Turkish steamer for Constantinople, the great metropolis that was a gateway between Europe and Asia, and for centuries the envy of both. Their boat passed many villages along the shore first colonized at the time of the ancient Greek migrations around the Euxine Sea. On the morning of the third day, the steamer entered the narrowing straits of the Bosporus, the gateway to the Black Sea, coveted by Jason and his argonauts as it was in later times by emperors, czars, and sultans. This fabled waterway forms the eastern boundary of the seagirt city, connecting with the Sea of Marmara to the south. Summer villas and palatial homes lined its hilly shores. On the right stood the vast marble and gold-leaf palace called Dolmabáçhe, a half mile in length. The Sultan who built it (Abdul-Medjid) gave orders that it must surpass in grandeur any palace of any potentate anywhere in the world. It was one of the last extravagant gestures of an empire suffering from a debauched and weakened leadership, though still the seat of the once-mighty Caliphate of Islam.

A forest of graceful minarets pierced the skies of this 'city of five hundred mosques', creating a splendid silhouette. Though capital of an empire of fading splendor, Constantinople was still, in 1863, an arrestingly beautiful city. Turkish architects who had revamped the Christian city had an eye for the natural contours, and viewing their city from the sea, sited their mosques as ornamentation for the natural rise of its seven hills.

Bahá'u'lláh's steamer entered the inlet of the Golden Horn, past the Grand Seraglio set amidst a mile-long park with its salons, courtyards, kiosks, terraces, gardens, and mosques. As they neared the harbor the Mosque of Suleiman the Magnificent rose before them, a token of the Ottoman empire's peak of glory. This greatest of Ottoman sultans had raised in the sixteenth century, with the genius of his architect, Sinan, magnificently beautiful mosques, hospitals, and schools on the hills that

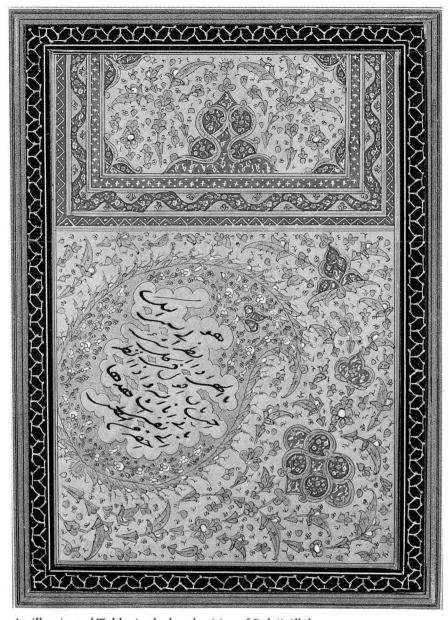

An illuminated Tablet in the handwriting of Bahá'u'lláh

When I contemplate, O my God, the relationship that bindeth me to Thee, I am moved to proclaim to all created things 'verily I am God!'; and when I consider my own self, lo, I find it coarser than clay!

were once the site of Constantine's New Rome.

But the Turks were not the first to recognize the strategic and aesthetic value of this window to East and West. Here Darius I once led his armies across the Bosporus to punish marauding tribes to the north at a time when Persia ruled the largest area in the world ever governed by one ruler. When, 'at God's command', Constantine the Great chose this spot, site of a Greek town called Byzantium, as the new capital of the Roman Empire, the weight of the whole Mediterranean world shifted from Italy to the East. Earlier he had placed his influence on the side of the Christians, claiming a vision of the cross in the sky as a sign of a coming military victory. Vision he assuredly had in choosing this exquisite spot for his New Rome. It was, wrote Gibbon, 'framed by Nature for the Centre and capital of a great monarch.'

Instead of New Rome it was soon named Constantinople. This also was, in Constantine's words, 'at God's command'. Surrounded on three sides by water and completely girt by mighty walls and ramparts, it remained impregnable for nearly twelve hundred years until the Turks finally captured it in 1453, with the exception of one brief hiatus in 1204 when it was occupied by envious Venetians and others under guise of a Crusade to the Holy Land.

Not far from the Turkish Palace of the Grand Seraglio (today a museum) there still stands the masterpiece of Byzantium architecture, envy and admiration of the Mediterranean world for centuries: the Hagia Sophia, Church of Divine Wisdom. It was raised in the sixth century by Justinian, Byzantium's famed maker of laws. When Constantinople finally yielded to the encircling Turkish power this Christian basilica was not destroyed or defaced, as were the beautiful mosques of Seville and Cordova by their Catholic conquerors in the same century. The architectural genius Sinan recognized it and its great dome as the zenith of architectural excellence of the age. Four tall minarets were added to convert it into a mosque. Today it still stands intact as a museum.

Doubtless Bahá'u'lláh knew the long history of the Hagia Sophia, then a mosque. His going forth in the city was confined almost entirely to visiting mosques, the public baths, and his brother's home during his brief sojourn there. At this time the Ottoman court was a hotbed of corruption, intrigue, and injustice, largely because of the misjudgment and weakness of the man who ruled as absolute monarch as well as Caliph of Islam – Sultan Abdul-Aziz. His empire was held together not so much through his own power as by the fact of being propped up by rival European powers, each determined not to let the prize that was Constantinople, the door to Asia, fall into its rivals' hands. The Sultan had a vacillating nature, veering from one extreme to the other. He lacked ability to select or direct adequately those who served under him. The great orientalist of Budapest, Professor Arminius Vambéry, said of him that he had the 'most contradictory character' of anyone he had known, a combination of 'generosity and meanness, cowardice and valor, shrewdness and ignorance, moderation and excess.'

One of history's interesting side-notes was this same Vambéry's meeting a half century later with 'Abdu'l-Bahá (long held a prisoner of the Sultanate) in Budapest, and his subsequent letter to him: 'Behind [your] ideals and deeds I easily discern the eternal welfare and prosperity of the world of humanity.' [11]

From the beginning of Bahá'u'lláh's arrival in the city, the Persian minister and his cohorts conspired with the Court to try to return him to Tehran that they might once more have him fully in their grasp. Officials of both governments called on Bahá'u'lláh, expecting him to seek favors and offer them bribes. Though courteous, Bahá'u'lláh did not return their visits, seek any advantages, or become involved in any of the affairs of court. When urged to do so he would say: 'I have come here at the Sultan's command. Whatsoever additional commands he may issue, I am ready to obey. My work is not of this world; it is of another realm, . . . Why, therefore, should I seek these people?'

They continued to seek him, however. Many of his visitors were so deeply impressed with his wisdom that his fame spread, attracting still others. The Persian minister at court grew increasingly discomfited and began to devise a plot to thwart Bahá'u'lláh's influence.

The Selim Mosque, whose graceful minarets dominate the skyline of Adrianople

8

A CALL
TO THE NATIONS

Within four months fresh orders came for further banishment to Adrianople on Turkey's remote western frontier bordering the European continent. Adrianople (Edirne to the Turks), named in the second century for the Roman Emperor Hadrian, was on the ancient land route between East and West even before Roman times. The journey was made in early December, again without adequate protection against the severe cold; it was said to be the worst winter in forty years and one that claimed the lives of many travelers.

From afar they could see the graceful minarets of the Selim Mosque, tallest of all Ottoman minarets and the most delicate in design of all Islam. It was Sinan's masterpiece. Here at last he had achieved his goal and 'with God's help . . . succeeded in building a dome . . . greater in diameter and higher than that of Hagia Sophia.' While Sinan contemplated his masterpiece and sought a way to wrest laurels from Christian architects, Michelangelo parried with popes in Rome and struggled to raise the dome of St. Peter's.

Whatever accusations concerning Bahá'u'lláh and his company – branding them as heretics and defamers of religion – may have reached the authorities in Adrianople or sifted down to the general population, they were soon dispelled. Their courtesy, gentleness, and acts of generosity belied any such epithets and won the confidence of the city's dwellers.

Seventy years later a very old man, recalling from boyhood his distinguished neighbors, especially Bahá'u'lláh and 'Abdu'l-Bahá, said to the American journalist Martha Root: 'They were very, very kind. They didn't harm anybody and they did good to everybody!'

For a time they dwelt in extremely cramped quarters. One day, with characteristic humor, Bahá'u'lláh said to a companion: 'You are a tall man and nearer to God. Pray that He may give us a better house.'[12] Within a few days the prayer was answered and a house was found near the Selim Mosque in the heart of the city.

The Válí, or Governor, as well as his deputy, called on Bahá'u'lláh. He developed a deep

attachment and admiration for Bahá'u'lláh and 'Abdu'l-Bahá. Visitors began to arrive from other lands, usually walking hundreds of miles. Some were sent forth again with the teachings of Bahá'u'lláh embedded in their hearts and minds, carrying messages to others, confirming those who awaited fulfillment of the Báb's promise as well as those who had not yet learned of the New Day. Several were seized and killed for the ardor of their faith and their audacity in sharing it with others.

It was to the rulers of the world that Bahá'u'lláh addressed his most compelling messages. Powerfully commanding, yet infinitely loving in tone, they summoned emperor and pope, caliph and king, high ecclesiastics of the East and West – they who held the well-being of the world's people in their hands. Like all mortal men, their days on earth were few, but their opportunity to heed the divine summons and to serve the world of humanity was unprecedented in all recorded history.

These messages, revealed both in Adrianople and later in 'Akká – some addressed individually, others collectively, to rulers, ecclesiastics, and others – urged those in power to come together and establish a World Federation whose members would take counsel together to arrive at a just and lasting peace among nations. He warned of the tragic results, the great and devastating wars to come should they prove heedless. With practical as well as idealistic counsel, he urged support of an international

police force to maintain peace between nations, thus reducing the excessive burden of armaments that hung upon the necks of the people. Each nation should maintain a disciplinary force consonant only with the need for internal order.

One of the responsibilities of the Federation would be to select an international auxiliary language to be taught in all schools of the world as an aid to better understanding, and a common script and currency to aid in world economy.

Bahá'u'lláh commended Queen Victoria for abolishing slavery throughout the British Empire, and for her actions in entrusting 'the reins of counsel into the hands of the representatives of the people', and concluded his message with a prayer for her guidance.

There were strong warnings. The German monarch was addressed with this remarkable vision of the future: 'Take warning, and be not of them that are fast asleep . . . O banks of the Rhine! We have seen you covered with gore, inasmuch as the swords of retribution were drawn against you; and you shall have another turn. And we hear the lamentations of Berlin, though she be today in conspicuous glory.'

He summoned the proud emperor, Napoleon III, to 'Arise . . . serve God and help His Cause . . . We have desired for thee naught except that which is better for thee than what thou dost possess and all the treasures of the earth.' These were days, he wrote, when 'the foundations of the cities have trembled, and the dust of irreligion hath enwrapped all men . . .' Jesus had earlier announced the coming of this new Light and now it was shining upon the world. It is said that Napoleon received this message with utter disdain.

Addressing the capital city of Sultan Abdul-Aziz, whose prisoner he was, Bahá'u'lláh wrote: 'We behold in thee the foolish ruling over the wise, and darkness vaunting itself against the light . . . Hath thine outward splendor made thee vainglorious? . . . It shall soon perish.'[13]

Even as these messages were being generated from this most significant spot where East and West meet, these two all-powerful monarchs of Orient and Occident consorted together in Paris. In July of 1867, before a grand review of artillery, cavalry, flying banners and martial music, Napoleon III and Abdul-Aziz appeared at the great International Exposition which had brought an unprecedented crowd of thousands to Paris from all over the world. Here is how one keen observer, noted American author Mark Twain, saw them:[14]

Napoleon . . . *such* a crafty scheming expression . . . bowing ever so gently to the loud plaudits, watching everything and everybody with his cat-eyes . . .

and

Abdul-Aziz . . . who holds in his hands the power of life and death over millions . . . who sees his people robbed and oppressed . . . but speaks no word to save them . . .

One cannot help but surmise, *where would the world be today had those two all-powerful monarchs of East and West, called all rulers to the council table and to peace?* Has any ruler ever stood at the portals of history with so great an opportunity to open the gates of freedom, prosperity, and peace for all mankind?

Strangely, these two monarchs were near relatives of a sort. The grandmother of Abdul-Aziz was a French girl, Aimée Dubucq de Rivery, whose cousin and best friend was Josephine, later the wife of Napoleon Bonaparte, uncle of Napoleon III. Returning to her family in Martinique from school in France, Aimée was captured by Algerian pirates and eventually presented to the Ottoman Sultan,

Abdul-Hamid I, in his later years. She became his favorite wife and wielded considerable power behind the throne. Eventually, against some odds, the 'French Sultana' as she was known, placed her son on the throne and became Queen Mother of the Ottoman Empire. Napoleon III once reminded the Sultan of this close family connection but Abdul-Aziz, it is said, was not amused.

It took only a decade to prove that Bahá'u'lláh's words were not void. But it was not surprising that the Sultan did not take kindly to the stern counsel of his Prisoner. Plans were soon afoot to increase the rigors of Bahá'u'lláh's exile.

From the time he set foot in Turkey Bahá'u'lláh's star began to ascend as he drew together the reins of his prophethood; but even as his Revelation increased in scope and power, so did his tribulations. It was not the threat of further banishment that cast the deepest shadows. Rather it was the treachery of the young half-brother whom he had reared and nurtured, whose envy had waxed greater as Bahá'u'lláh's influence grew. He sought every means of creating conflict and misunderstanding, not only among the believers but among government and religious authorities at the capital. With a few henchmen he plotted attempts on the life of Bahá'u'lláh.

Bahá'u'lláh was long-suffering, making every effort to cool the jealousy that raged in his brother's heart, but the final rift was inevitable. It brought turmoil and confusion into the ranks of his companions and precipitated action from the government. It was the greatest sorrow of Bahá'u'lláh's life. Even though two other brothers remained devoted and faithful and shared his exile from the beginning, it did not erase the scars of this infamy. It was Cain and Abel once again.

Aerial view of the city of 'Akká

9

TO THE
DESOLATE CITY

The new order came from the Sultan: perpetual banishment and life imprisonment for Bahá'u'-lláh, his family, and close followers in the Turkish penal colony of 'Akká in Palestine. They were to be incarcerated in the Citadel, the mammoth prison-barracks built by the Turks in about 1819 on the site of the main castle of the Crusader Knights of St. John.

It was, wrote Bahá'u'lláh, 'the most desolate of the cities of the world'! He called it 'the metropolis of the owl.'

And desolate it was in the mid-nineteenth century: known as a pestilential city, given to plagues and epidemics, with no clean water supply within its gates. It had known far better times and once possessed the finest harbor on the whole coast of the eastern Mediterranean.

The stones of 'Akká and the sands of its shores carry the memoried imprints of civilizations long past. Besieged again and again, it is said that more blood has flowed on this shore than on any other spot on earth. To this region the Hebrew tribe of Asher was sent. Unlike many of the tribes sent forth by Joshua and the Jewish leaders, they did not drive out the inhabitants. Rather, according to the ancient scribe of Judges, they 'dwelt among the Canaanites, the inhabitants of the land'.

Long before Asher the culture of Sumeria, of Mesopotamia, and of Egypt was exchanged and absorbed as the thrust of civilization shifted back and forth according to the tides of fortune. From this eastern coast of the Middle Sea, seafaring Phoenicians sailed their galleys laden with the arts and wares of neighboring lands. Among the 'goods' they distributed was an alphabet developed by the culturally fertile peoples of the Near East.

Persian, Greek, Roman, Byzantine, and Arab each had a day of victory and a day of defeat on this soil. 'Akká was named Ptolemais for the dynasty that ruled Egypt after the death of Alexander the Great, until Cleopatra capitulated to Rome and to romance.

When Christian Crusaders came from Europe to regain the Holy Land for Christendom about AD 1100, they renamed the city St. Jean d'Acre for the Order of the Knights of St. John who headquartered there. Soon it became the chief seaport of the new kingdom and the ships of all Europe entered its harbor and plied the Mediterranean with the exotic riches of the East. With a divisiveness that plagued Christendom almost from its beginnings, the city was divided up among rival camps of Venetians, Pisans, Genoans, Germans, English, and French. When the warriors of Saladin administered a decisive defeat in 1187 to the Crusader army, the Christian capital was moved from Jerusalem to St. Jean d'Acre, until the Crusaders were eventually driven entirely from their foothold in the Holy Land. Meanwhile, both the Order of the Knights Templar, who had lost their stronghold

in Jerusalem near the site of Solomon's Temple, and the Knights of St. John carried on an intense rivalry that often erupted into violence – though both wore the Christian cross, symbol of peace, upon their vestments.

In the late thirteenth century, young Marco Polo of Venice, with his father and uncle, set out from 'Akká on a journey that made them history's most celebrated tourists. Across the Lebanese hills, through Mesopotamia, Persia, and the Gobi desert, they came finally to fabled Cathay, the realm of Kublai Khan.

In the early sixteenth century Palestine became part of the Ottoman Empire which was to stretch from the Balkans in Europe to the Persian Gulf, one of the world's largest, most

powerful, and long-lasting empires, and one that for many years sent tremors of fear throughout Europe. Now, even the far reaches of the empire felt the erratic rule of the fear-haunted, tyrannical Sultan in whose hands the destiny of Bahá'u'lláh was seemingly held.

The day of departure for Bahá'u'lláh drew near. The Governor of Adrianople had tried in vain to intervene on his behalf. Members of European consulates called daily at his home, offering assistance. To all he extended gracious thanks but declined to take advantage of their goodwill. More than anyone, he knew that his Mission must move on to its ultimate destiny. A four-day land journey with military escort brought the band of exiles to Gallipoli – Calli-

polis of ancient Thrace. The strict surveillance of the captain who led the military guard melted during those days into a strong attachment for his captives. To Bahá'u'lláh, he extended apologies for the role he had to play.

'Tell the king,' said Bahá'u'lláh, 'that this territory will pass out of his hands, and his affairs will be thrown into confusion.'

Bahá'ís not destined for the penal colony offered the authorities to pay their own way if only they could accompany Bahá'u'lláh to the prison. The sea voyage, beginning on Friday, 21 August 1868, took eleven days with stops at Smyrna, and at Alexandria and Port Said in Egypt. Toward Sunday evening the exiles caught their first glimpse of the Palestinian shore, land of their fourth and final banishment.

Sunset cast a glow on the harbor of Jaffa (Yafo), ancient gateway to the sea since the cedars of Lebanon had flowed through it for Solomon's temple in Jerusalem. It reflected upon the Franciscan monastery high on the cliff and on a little mosque nearby, believed to be the site of the home of Simon the tanner where Peter stayed. A myriad ancient memories and myths lingered in the historical mists. From here Jonah is said to have left on his extraordinary voyage and encounter with the ocean leviathan as he tried to escape the Lord's bidding to go to Nineveh. Twice in three centuries the sea mingled with the tears of escaping Jews: once in 166 BC when the Greeks took revenge for the Maccabean victory, and again in AD 70 when Rome sacked the city.

Here the Crusaders jubilantly *en route* to Jerusalem devoutly kissed the ground, their first contact with terra sancta. What hopes, what joys were poured forth as thousands of booted and

View from 'Akká to Haifa at sunset

sandled feet trod city stones and desert sands on their way to Jerusalem, the way to salvation!

What must have been the thoughts and feelings that surged through the mind and heart of Bahá'u'lláh as he gazed upon this land? Surely he thought of the Prophets of old, of Moses, of Jesus, of Muhammad. Shrouded in mystery, this land of the Prophets has profoundly affected all humankind throughout recorded history. Tradition and eastern texts say that Zoroaster consorted with the Hebrew prophets here; that Socrates once came from Greece and from the same source found his philosophical roots and belief in the immortality of the soul.

At midnight the steamer moved on again as only the beam of the lighthouse and a few twinkling lights marked the shore. With the first streaks of dawn Mount Carmel came into view. *Did Bahá'u'lláh already know in his heart that the Mountain of Elijah would be the final resting-place for the Báb, the youthful Precursor of his own Revelation?*

After hours of waiting onshore in Haifa, they were crowded into a sailing vessel that drifted slowly around the bay toward 'Akká. It was a hot, windless day. The old city seemed to be floating on the water with the great Citadel looming ominously on the left. Nearby rose the white dome of the al-Jazzar Mosque, the largest in Palestine, named for the Pasha who had repelled Bonaparte's siege of 1799. Camel riders rode along the shallow sandy shore. Farther out white waves beat a froth against the ruins of a Crusader tower jutting above the water, evoking thoughts of Richard the Lion-Hearted and Saladin. Heavy stone walls with their gun turrets lined the shore.

The boat entered the harbor as the narrow sea gate was opened. A menacing crowd of onlookers moved in more closely. Turkish guards barked their orders and started the exiles on the long walk through the winding market

street, past the al-Jazzar Mosque, to the prison gates, subject all the time to rude stares and shouted insults.

For Bahá'u'lláh and for many in his company the long trail of exile was ended. In the prophetic words of Micah, he had come 'from the fortified cities . . . from sea to sea, and from mountain to mountain'. Although twenty-four years of his Mission still lay ahead and many of his greatest works were yet to be revealed, his dust would one day rest in this Holy Land that had known the footsteps of so many Prophets of God.

For one young man the far future held in store long journeys filled with wondrous events. After a lifetime of exile, prison, and the onslaught of many tribulations and perils, and with no formal schooling, he would travel to the West. In Paris, London, New York, Montreal, Chicago, San Francisco, and a host of other cities, thousands would come to hear him speak. Both high and low, from many walks of life, would seek his counsel. Even the Western journalists who covered his visit would accord him a rare honor and respect which his dignity and wisdom, his simplicity and gentle humor seemed to evoke. He was 'Abdu'l-Bahá, twenty-four years of age as he entered the great prison, and already becoming the chief cornerstone of his father's Faith.

10

LIGHT FROM
A PRISON CELL

She was small and dainty in appearance, gently reared, her large, grey-blue eyes calm but ever alert in the piquant face. Though gentle in manner and compassionate by nature, she possessed unwavering courage and an iron strength forged through twenty-two years of hardship and cruelty. She was Bahíyyih Khánum and when she was born in Tehran in 1846 her father, Bahá'u'lláh, was already the fearless champion of the Báb's Cause.

Throughout her long life Bahíyyih Khánum recalled the fearful days in Tehran when her father was held in the Black Pit and the threatening mobs circled their home. She was six years old when they left Tehran on the winter road of exile to Baghdad. Most vividly of all in her memory was etched her first sight of the barracks room in 'Akká as the great, heavy doors were slammed and bolted behind them.

'I cannot find words to describe the filth and stench of that vile place,' she said in her late years.

They huddled together on the damp, earthen floor in the heavy heat, some seventy men, women and children. Hungry, nearly perishing from thirst after eight hours in hot sun in the open sailing vessel, they were given no food or water that first night, and later only black, salty bread and filthy, brackish water. In the coming weeks almost the entire company fell ill with typhoid, dysentery, and malaria. No physician, no medicine was permitted to them. It was 'Abdu'l-Bahá who, somehow managing to stay well, cared for the others and nursed them back to health, all except three who died in those early weeks of nightmare.

Today the sodden floors and filthy conditions no longer exist. Part of the massive structure is a museum, part once served as a mental institution. But the cell of Bahá'u'lláh on the upper level later assigned to him, is still preserved, having been recognized as a Bahá'í Holy Place for half a century. It is a place of visitation for Bahá'í pilgrims who come to the Holy Land. The iron gate is opened and the pilgrim enters the barren cell, a stark contrast to the serene beauty of Bahjí. He crosses the room to a

window on the west and looks out over the rooftops at the walled ramparts that remain and the waves rolling incessantly to the shore. It looks much the same as it must have looked to Bahá'u'lláh over a century ago. But now there is no lone figure in robe and turban by the distant wall beyond the outer moat, standing motionless and gazing at the little window of the prison, hoping that Bahá'u'lláh might catch sight of him and know of his love and loyalty.

Today, borne swiftly by jet plane, modern pilgrims come in a few hours from all parts of the globe. In this prison cell, more than any other place he will visit, the pilgrim is borne even more swiftly backward in time to the day when Bahá'u'lláh and the company of exiles arrived at this grim fortress, when just the effort to see him or to enter the prison-city could bring imprisonment or swift death.

They came in ones and twos, those first pilgrims, traveling mostly on foot the hundreds of precarious miles from Persia or Iraq, through areas infested with brigands and highwaymen. Many returned again to their native land after only a brief glimpse of the beloved figure behind the barred window. Some found a refuge in nearby towns and eked out a bare livelihood. Some lived in caves.

Among the first few pilgrims was a youth of seventeen who had been deeply stirred by the teachings of Bahá'u'lláh. To meet him face to face became his sole desire in life. Traveling all the way on foot, he arrived in 'Akká where, dressed as a water carrier, he was able to enter the prison and see Bahá'u'lláh. Eagerly he accepted the mission of carrying back a letter to the Shah, fully aware of the personal risk involved even in trying to approach that haughty tyrant. Alone, unaided, he accomplished his difficult task. Needless to say, the proud, despotic Nasr-ed-Din Shah did not reply to the letter sent to him by Bahá'u'lláh. The young man who bore the message was seized, tortured, and went to his death refusing to reveal the names of fellow believers, smiling at his tormentors who were at a loss to comprehend the source of his dauntlessness. Today Bahá'í youth the world over look upon Badí' (Wonderful), as Bahá'u'lláh named him, as an example of both physical and moral courage.

Life in the Turkish Bastille, as it was called, was bleak and severe, even for the hardened criminals who made up most of the inmates. For people who had been gently reared, as were Bahá'u'lláh and his family, living conditions were harsh in the extreme, even when compared to the years of exile and deprivation they had already sustained. Calamities occurred almost daily, one in particular bringing excruciating sorrow. A son of Bahá'u'lláh, the younger brother of 'Abdu'l-Bahá, who was beloved for his kind and reverent nature, fell from a prison skylight as he paced the roof saying his evening prayers. To his father he spoke the wish that he might give his life as a ransom for the believers who wanted so desperately to be allowed to visit Bahá'u'lláh.

In spite of the austere, often brutish conditions of life, and the inadequate food allowance,

Sea front in 'Akká with view of the House of 'Abbúd (white house) where Bahá'u'lláh resided for six years

there were many moments of joy and laughter. The companions of Bahá'u'lláh were there by choice, preferring prison with him to freedom on the outside and what had been for some a life of ease. They sang songs, chanted prayers, told stories, and made light of their hardships. Often their laughter rang throughout the prison, producing astonishment in the minds of the prison guards.

'What kind of prisoners are these?' they asked each other.

They were peaceful, friendly, courteous, and spent much time in words of gratitude and praise to God. *How could they be guilty of perverting the religion of God?* One official came to interview Bahá'u'lláh shortly after his incarceration. Another prisoner, witnessing the interview, recorded it thus:

'[Bahá'u'lláh] spoke such words of knowledge and wisdom,' he said, 'that, in that very first meeting, they realized that here were people endowed with erudition, wisdom and rare understanding.'

Over forty years later in London, 'Abdu'l-Bahá, freed at last by the Young Turk revolution, was asked about his prison life.

'I was happy in that prison, for those days were passed in the path of service,' he said. 'When one is released from the prison of self, that is indeed freedom! For self is the greatest prison . . . Unless one accepts dire vicissitudes, not with dull resignation, but with radiant acquiescence, one cannot attain this freedom.'

While the officials and guards in 'Akká took note of their unusual charges, the work of Bahá'u'lláh went on apace. In the midst of the rigors of prison life, the need each day to counsel and console his companions, to consult with his beloved elder son, who, then only twenty-four years of age, bore such heavy burdens of responsibility, some of Bahá'u'lláh's most important messages were revealed.

To the Pope in Rome, he wrote that the time had come for the great ingathering of the people of the world foretold by Christ. 'Incline thine ear unto that which the Fashioner of mouldering bones counselleth thee,' he wrote. 'Sell all the embellished ornaments thou dost possess, and expend them in the path of God, Who causeth the night to return upon the day, and the day to return upon the night.'

To the Czar of Russia he announced the advent of the Father, he whom Isaiah had foretold, and 'with Whose name both the Torah and the Evangel were adorned . . .'

From his cell a second letter was sent to Napoleon III who had cast aside the first one with disdain. 'Hath thy pomp made thee proud?' Bahá'u'lláh asked. 'It shall not endure . . . thy kingdom shall be thrown into confusion, and thine empire shall pass from thine hands . . .'

For Napoleon, secure and arrogant in his power, the battle of Sedan was only months away, destined to bring him total defeat, shocking the entire world.

With only bare walls and barred windows to greet his eyes each day, and with the Sultan's decree hanging over him like a sword on a silken thread, Bahá'u'lláh nevertheless foretold that one day he would pitch his tent upon Mount Carmel, that Mountain of God which Isaiah wrote would one day 'see the glory of the Lord'.

'Fear not,' he said. 'These doors shall be opened. My tent shall be pitched on Mount Carmel, and the utmost joy shall be realized.'

The House of 'Abbúd in 'Akká

The Khan al-'Umdan (Inn of the Pillars) in 'Akká, a caravanserai where early Bahá'í pilgrims stayed

Mazra'ih, a house in the country which became Bahá'u'lláh's first residence outside the walls of the prison-city of 'Akká. The aqueduct can be seen leading from the reservoir at center right.

Old aqueduct near 'Akká, once restored at the suggestion of Bahá'u'lláh

11

A FOUNTAIN
OF LIVING WATERS

Traveling a few kilometers north of 'Akká on the Nahariya road, a tall arched ruin suddenly looms against the sky, making one think for a moment that he has been transported to the Italian *campagna*. At times the arches rise double upon their supporting pillars reaching a height of ten meters. It is an old aqueduct built two centuries ago by the Turkish governor Ahmad Pasha, known as al-Jazzar (Cut-throat) for his cruelty. He ruled from 1775 to 1804, and the aqueduct which brought fresh water to the inhabitants of 'Akká was one of the better accomplishments of Turkish rule in Palestine. With British help, al-Jazzar managed to thwart Napoleon Bonaparte's thrust to capture 'Akká as a wedge for subduing Turkey and making it a gateway to India. Some of the results of the bombardment are still visible. Among the casualties was al-Jazzar's aqueduct, though it was later rebuilt and repaired several times.

The source of water for the aqueduct was the springs of Kabri, near a village thirteen kilometers to the northeast of 'Akká, an area abundant with natural fountains bubbling from the ground. Signs remain at Kabri that tell the story of ancient wells that furnished fresh water for villagers long centuries before it was channeled into al-Jazzar's aqueduct. At the time of Bahá'u'lláh's coming to 'Akká in 1868 the wells no longer served a useful purpose for the people of 'Akká, for the aqueduct had been in a state of disrepair for nearly thirty years.

This man-made waterway, now again largely in ruins, has a special significance for Bahá'ís. It represents an event in the life of Bahá'u'lláh illustrative of a power that dwelt within him and that surrounded his entire ministry. It was more than the quality of an exalted character which he inherently possessed. It was a spirit from God which, like 'a pillar of cloud by day and [a] pillar of fire by night', had guided him to this land above and beyond his own purposiveness. It drew the souls of the pure in heart to him like moth to candle and often changed the hearts of bitter foes into well-wishers. The Báb had manifested this power abundantly and it was increasingly evinced in the life of 'Abdu'l-Bahá as his unique station in the Faith of his father evolved.

From the beginning the Sultan had laid down severe rules concerning Bahá'u'lláh and the exiles. To make certain that no sympathy be shown them his firman was read in the great al-Jazzar Mosque shortly after their arrival, apprising the congregation of their 'crimes against religion'. A man of some standing in the community listened to the charges and became so wrought up that he made plans to visit Bahá'u'lláh and take his life. His plans were frustrated several times, but the visit finally took place. Then, instead of being overcome with hatred, the man was overwhelmed with the prisoner's wisdom and compassion and found himself desiring only to become a devoted follower.

Two years after the arrival of the exiles, the movement of Turkish troops in the unstable Ottoman Empire necessitated the full use of the Citadel as a military barracks. Although the exiles continued to be treated as prisoners and to remain within the confines of the penal colony, they were placed here and there in various houses in the city. Bahá'u'lláh and his family were forced to move four times, finally coming to live in what is known as the House of 'Abbúd close by the sea wall. Here he resided the last six years that he spent within the walls of the prison-city and here his most important work, the Book of Laws, was revealed.

District governors, or pashas, came and went in the Sultan's shaky administration. Each generally began his term with a determination to enforce strictly the Sultan's firman in respect of the exiles. Later they would come to know 'Abdu'l-Bahá. The noble bearing that was his natural mien, the geniality and kindliness that radiated from him, often proved irresistible. Through 'Abdu'l-Bahá they learned of the true teachings of Bahá'u'lláh. Frequently, though not always, animosity changed into admiration and friendship. The lesser among them were content to accept the calumniation at face value and to seek personal advantages.

There was a governor among them named Ahmad Big Tawfiq. Antagonists of Bahá'u'lláh had presented him with some of his writings with a view to arousing his wrath against the exiles. Instead, the words held an attraction for him. He wanted to learn more. He sought out 'Abdu'l-Bahá and listened intently to his explanations. A deep respect emerged in his mind, growing into profound admiration and friendship. He beseeched 'Abdu'l-Bahá for a personal interview with his father, forgetting for the moment that Bahá'u'lláh was actually his prisoner and at his command. The meeting took place and the Governor pleaded with Bahá'u'lláh to be allowed to perform some special service for him.

Bahá'u'lláh's answer astonished the Governor. It was not what one would expect from a prisoner confined to a penal colony and subject to harsh restrictions. Bahá'u'lláh did not ask for release nor for any special favors for himself or his companions.

'Restore the aqueduct that fresh water may once again flow freely into the city and benefit the health of all,' was the essence of the response given to the Governor.

The request was quickly carried out. Soon fresh spring water from Kabri was once again flowing into 'Akká. The health of the population improved considerably and the debilitating epidemics diminished.

The townspeople watched and pondered these unusual prisoners in their midst. They saw 'Abdu'l-Bahá come forth daily into the streets to alleviate the material and spiritual needs of the people, especially those of the poor. Many, high

and low, sought his counsel in the perplexities and difficulties of their lives. Most of the populace, perhaps, did not consciously associate their improved well-being with Bahá'u'lláh or even with the reconstructed aqueduct. Yet many of them, who, a few short years earlier, had stared with enmity and shouted threats as the exiles arrived on their shores, now felt a special beneficence from their presence among them.

The *fountain of living water*, in Jeremiah's words, was flowing freely both spiritually and materially in their very midst. Today the aqueduct is only an interesting historic ruin, no longer needed for practical purposes with the new and modern water system that has been established. But to Bahá'ís it has a special meaning as a symbol of the power and compassion of Bahá'u'lláh.

In the path of the aqueduct lies the house with its gardens, known as Mazra'ih. It is located about ten kilometers north of 'Akká and it was Bahá'u'lláh's first dwelling place after his historic departure from the confines of the penal colony. The same radiant qualities of soul that had drawn the friendly Governor and others were instrumental in this profound change in the outward conditions of his life.

The walls of his cell, the walls of the prison-city and beyond them the endless sea had encompassed his outer range of vision for nearly nine years. For one who from childhood had felt deep kinship with nature, and in boyhood had roamed country fields and wooded hills, 'Akká was indeed the 'metropolis of the owl'. His love of the wonders of creation and the natural world was evident in his writings. From trees and woodlands, rippling streams and mountains, flowers and birds, he drew symbols for expressing spiritual truths, drawing his loved ones nearer to the ever-hidden essence of the beauty of God.

'Every created thing in the whole universe', he revealed, 'is but a door leading into His knowledge, a sign of His sovereignty, a revelation of His names, a symbol of His majesty, a token of His power, a means of admittance into His straight Path . . .'

The Revelation of God, and all the qualities of

the spirit, are expressed in metaphors involving the world of creation. God's Revelation, poured forth in every age through His Prophet, is a 'river of everlasting life', 'streams flowing from . . . all glorious heights'. God's love, mercy, and forgiveness are as 'seas of loving-kindness', an 'ocean of mercy', 'gentle gales of pardon and grace'. The need of the human spirit to rise and soar upward toward its Creator is expressed as the 'bird of the heart'; and hope and spiritual renewal themselves come to the soul as the 'dawning place of inspiration', 'the morn of . . . endless favor'. Humanity he likened to a garden, its different plants, flowers, fruits all precious and needed for the well-being and beauty of the whole. Children especially were the 'roses of [God's] garden', 'the flowers of [His] meadows'.

That the human side of Bahá'u'lláh's nature, so long confined by prison walls and the walls of the penal colony, once again longed to commune freely with nature, to reflect upon its beauties, and to absorb its healing qualities, was apparent. One day he said with obvious yearning: 'The country is the world of the soul, the city is the world of bodies.'

As soon as 'Abdu'l-Bahá heard these words, he did not rest until he was able to find a house in the country, called Mazra'ih, surrounded by gardens and with a small stream, a mile from the sea. But when the time came to tell Bahá'u'lláh about Mazra'ih and that all was in readiness for him, he would not leave 'Akká. 'I am a prisoner,' he said. It was true, the Sultan's firman had never been rescinded, though Abdul-Aziz was by this time dethroned and had lost his life.

The Mufti of 'Akká pleaded with him. He was not a follower of Bahá'u'lláh but he respected him and loved him deeply. 'Who has the power to make you a prisoner?' he asked.

Finally Bahá'u'lláh consented to go. The words proved true, for no one, not even the guards at the city gates, raised a hand to prevent his departure from the confines of the penal colony.

Another small retreat was secured for him, a tiny island garden nearby. It became his favorite

Stairway at Mazra'ih leading to Bahá'u'lláh's room

spot, known as the Garden of Riḍván as is the one in Baghdad where the great festival of Bahá'u'lláh's Declaration had taken place. Here on this tiny refuge was a small house where he sometimes rested.

Both Mazra'ih, today beautifully restored and surrounded by gardens, and the green haven of the Riḍván Garden with its fountain, running water, mulberry trees and singing birds, as well as his room preserved in the little house, are places of pilgrimage for Bahá'ís. The joyful release that Bahá'u'lláh felt in this charming country setting seems still to pervade the atmosphere. The valley, the hills, the open fields and streams of his youth were echoed once again in his life these latter years. Here he lived for two years, and then a cholera epidemic swept the area. The Mansion of Bahjí nearby was hastily abandoned by its owner and 'Abdu'l-Bahá was able to secure it for his father at very small cost. Thus Bahjí became Bahá'u'lláh's last home and the site of his resting-place, supremely sacred to his followers.

The fountain, and the bench where Bahá'u'lláh sometimes sat, in the Garden of Ridván.

Haste thee, O Carmel, for lo, the light of the countenance of God, the Ruler of the Kingdom of Names and Fashioner of the heavens, hath been lifted upon thee.

From Bahá'u'lláh's Tablet of Carmel

12

THE MAJESTY
OF CARMEL

'. . . *the majesty of Carmel and Sharon, they shall see the glory of the Lord,* . . .' extolled Isaiah.

It was not Isaiah who chose and exalted this spot. But it was his vision and gift of prophecy that encompassed not only the natural charm of this setting with the mountain range curving into the blue sea, but also especially its future glory.

Carmel was known in ancient times as a fruitful place, its slopes nurturing vineyards and gardens. More significantly it sheltered many of the holy ones of God, until today it has become the resting-place of the Báb, he who prepared the way for the coming of the Glory of God, Bahá'u'lláh. Its very name, formed from a Hebrew word *Cerem-El*, means 'the Vineyard of God'.

Elijah dwelt in its caves. Here he chastised the Israelites for falling into idolatry, and proved the ascendancy of the God of Abraham and Moses over the materialistic priests of Baal. Here Elisha went for a time after the mantle of Elijah fell upon him. Solomon sang of its beauty. Surely Jesus knew Carmel, little more than a day's foot journey from his home in Nazareth. Even the Greeks who lived on this Palestinian shore long before Roman times held it as a place favored by gods and heroes. It was Herodotus, the 'father of history', who portrayed the mystic philosopher Pythagoras descending the mountain to his ship below.

Standing in front of the Shrine of the Báb today one looks down the nine landscaped terraces leading to Carmel Avenue* and to the harbor. The avenue not only points the way to the entrance of the Shrine but also across the bay to 'Akká, and beyond 'Akká to Bahjí and the Shrine of Bahá'u'lláh. It is as if this street were laid out to serve as a line of orientation from Shrine to Shrine, visible from mountain, sea, or sky.

Once Carmel was the main avenue of the German colony known as the Templars who migrated to the Holy Land near the time of Bahá'u'lláh's coming. The German Templars

* Now Ben-Gurion Avenue.

did much to develop the town of Haifa and its environs in the half-century of their sojourn there. Along the avenue can be seen their white stone houses with red-tiled roofs, some of them over a hundred years old. One of the homes is today the Hotel Appinger, named for the family who built it.

They were not the first of their countrymen to settle in the Holy Land. Seven hundred years earlier some German merchants had come to 'Akká and established a hospital which evolved into the Order of Teutonic Knights, a military order open only to Germans. But the settlers of the mid-nineteenth century had little in common with their countrymen of an earlier time. They did not come to conquer the people or the land. They came, in the words of Isaiah, to 'see the glory of the Lord'. They came with the conviction that the second coming of their Lord was imminent, that only a reformed and spiritualized Christian community would be a fitting body to receive him when he appeared. Their hopes and expectations can still be seen in the inscriptions carved over their doorways, *Der Herr ist nahe* (the Lord is near) being one.

Over the years, more than a thousand German Templars migrated to the Holy Land, the majority settling in the region of Haifa. They were mostly farmers and craftsmen, people accustomed to hard, honest labor. Accordingly they laid out their new colony at the foot of Carmel, then nearly a mile from the small village of Haifa where Bahá'u'lláh had landed briefly on the way to 'Akká. Here they built their sturdy houses, planted gardens and olive groves and vineyards in a wasted and desolate land. With no knowledge of climate, soil, language, or customs of the inhabitants, they persevered against severe hardships for many years. In time they overcame much of the suspicion and resentment of the native Arabs and helped them to improve their farming methods. They pioneered wagon trails and roads to other towns, having introduced the use of wheeled vehicles for transportation. Eventually, during the British Mandate control of the Holy Land, most of the colony dispersed and resettled in other parts of the

The Shrine of the Báb, overlooking the houses of the former German Templar colony that line the avenue below

world.

In the bosom of Carmel, close by the Shrine of the Báb, stands a small circular grove of cypress trees. Photographs at the turn of the century show this grove surrounded by boulders and rocky soil with little vegetation. The trees were planted by one of the German gardeners who many years later worked for 'Abdu'l-Bahá in the initial work of beautifying Carmel. The purpose of the planting is not known – whether to develop vegetation and counteract erosion on the slope, or for beauty and shade, or if, deep in his heart, he thought that perchance his Lord would come and seek shelter there from the heat of the day.

Today the trees remain, protected by a low circular wall and path. They stand like sentinels on the slope just above the Shrine of the Báb. Instead of stony, thorny land they are surrounded by beautiful gardens.

This little grove of trees is a hallowed spot to Bahá'ís. Here beneath their shade Bahá'u'lláh rested for a time to view the surrounding area. Here he pointed out to 'Abdu'l-Bahá where the Shrine of the Báb should be built. *For Bahá'u'lláh had indeed pitched his tent on Carmel, as he had foretold from the prison*, not once but several times. On the last occasion, a year before his passing in 1892, he remained for three months. Once his tent stood near the house with the inscription, *Der Herr ist nahe.*

What thoughts must have coursed through the mind of 'Abdu'l-Bahá at this time! Since a small boy his every thought and purpose had been to carry out the wishes of his father. They were still prisoners of the Turkish government. How could the land for the site be secured? How could a fitting structure be raised? How indeed could the remains of the Báb so cautiously protected for decades in Persia be brought the long, precarious route to the Holy Land? It would be eighteen years before the prodigious task could be accomplished. These were years

when 'Abdu'l-Bahá shouldered alone the burden of leadership bestowed upon him in the Testament written by his father. Under the chaotic Sultanate of Abdul-Hamid II he would again be subjected to fresh trials and calamities, once more incarcerated, his very life often hanging in the balance – years that strained his strength and capacity to the fullest.

'Every stone of that building,' he later said of the Shrine, 'every stone of the road leading to it, I have with infinite tears and at tremendous cost, raised . . .'

It was one of three major tasks he assumed during the years he served as the Center of Bahá'u'lláh's Covenant, the point of unity for the Bahá'ís of East and West, and the appointed interpreter of his father's writings. Another was the establishment of the Bahá'í Faith in the West, to which his historic journey to Europe and America, made in his late years, so greatly contributed.

But now all was joy and victory on the Mountain of God! Here Bahá'u'lláh revealed his famed *Tablet of Carmel* that would make for all time that holy mountain the world center of the Faith he had established.

' "Haste thee, O Carmel, for lo, the light of the countenance of God, the Ruler of the Kingdom of Names and Fashioner of the heavens, hath been lifted upon thee." ' . . . 'Rejoice, for God hath in this Day established upon thee His throne . . .' And again, 'Call out to Zion, O Carmel, and announce the joyful tidings: He that was hidden from mortal eyes is come! . . . Oh, how I long to announce unto every spot on the surface of the earth, and to carry to each one of its cities, the glad-tidings of this Revelation . . .'

Bahá'u'lláh would not carry the glad-tidings to the cities of the earth. But 'Abdu'l-Bahá would. And after him there would be others – a few, then hundreds, thousands who would go forth to cover the earth with the knowledge of God 'as the waters cover the sea'.

Cypress trees behind the Shrine of the Báb

The Bahá'í Temple, Wilmette, Illinois, overlooking Lake Michigan near Chicago

Metro Aerial Photos

13

TO BUILD
A TABERNACLE
OF PEACE

Behold the man whose name is The Branch
. . . he shall build the temple of the Lord.

Zechariah 6 : 12

In a secluded corner of a garden near the Shrine of the Báb there stands a tall, white, lace-like panel – a casting of concrete and quartz that forms a kind of filigreed arch. It is a section of the exterior ornamentation from the world-renowned Bahá'í Temple situated on the shore of Lake Michigan near Chicago in suburban Wilmette. Even prior to its dedication in 1953, this House of Worship had drawn many thousands of visitors to its portals from all over the world. Visitors to the Shrine of the Báb in Haifa frequently say: 'We have visited your beautiful Temple in Chicago!'

Many who call themselves Bahá'ís first learned of their Faith from this great 'silent teacher', as it is called. In the beginning when the design was first displayed, some observers called it 'the temple of light'. The sunlight streams in through the great dome and the nine-sided lacy interior. At night the light from within penetrates the surrounding darkness, symbolic, Bahá'ís believe, of the spiritual meaning of the Temple. People of many faiths and of no formal religion come here to pray and meditate in the serene atmosphere it invokes.

Over the archways both inside and out are inscribed selected writings of Bahá'u'lláh, eighteen in all, such as the following:

So powerful is unity's light that it can illumine the
*   whole earth.*
Consort with the followers of all religions with
*   friendliness.*
The source of all learning is the knowledge of
*   God . . .*
All the Prophets of God proclaim the same Faith.

When the model for this 'temple of light' was first shown in a New York gallery, it evoked considerable stir among architects, artists, journalists, and others.

'It is the first new idea in architecture since the 13th century,' stated the President of the Architectural League.

A European professor of architecture from Turin observed: 'Without doubt it will have a lasting page in history. It is a revelation from another world.'

BAHÁ'Í TEMPLES

Wilmette, Illinois, USA

Kampala, Uganda

Sydney, Australia

Frankfurt, Germany

BAHÁ'Í WORSHIP

The purpose of a House of Worship is to bring men and women together in unity. 'For thousands of years the human race has been at war. It is enough . . . For thousands of years the nations have denied each other, considering each other as infidel and inferior. It is sufficient. We must now realize that we are the servants of one God, that we turn to one beneficent Father, live under one divine law, seek one reality and have one desire. Thus may we live in the utmost friendship and love, and in return the favors and bounties of God shall surround us, the world of humanity will be reformed, mankind enjoy a new life. . .' ('Abdu'l-Bahá)

The auditorium of the Temple is open to all people for prayer and meditation. No race or religion is barred. Services are not elaborate. There is no ritualism or set form. Services are for prayer, meditation, and the reading of selections from the Sacred Scriptures of the Bahá'í Faith and the other great Faiths of the world.

New Delhi, India

Panama City, Panama

Apia, Western Samoa

Newspapers around the world carried the story. In Tokyo a newspaper featured it as the 'Temple of Peace, whose broad portals of welcome and encouragement to devotees of any religion, and all religions, shall be always open.'

The nine sides of this House of Worship, symbolic of unity and all-inclusiveness, are a unique architectural feature fundamental to all Bahá'í temples already existing or in the process of being raised, in Europe, Africa, Latin America, Australia, India, and the South Pacific.

Early in the development of the Bahá'í Faith in America, the believers there longed to construct an edifice worthy of the universal and lofty ideals of their Faith. They were few in number and limited in funds. Mrs. Corinne True, an early American Bahá'í, traveled to the Holy Land in 1907 with a petition seeking 'Abdu'l-Bahá's blessing and guidance for their endeavor.

'Make a beginning,' he encouraged, 'and all will come right.'

In a very few years 'Abdu'l-Bahá himself was to come to America to lay the cornerstone of this 'mother temple' of the Bahá'í world. Freed at last from the Turkish yoke that had held him in bondage for over forty years, and with the remains of the Báb safely entombed in the mausoleum in the heart of Carmel, he turned his face to his next vital objective: *establishing the Faith of Bahá'u'lláh in the West.*

'From the beginning of time until the present day,' he observed, 'the light of Divine Revelation hath risen in the East and shed its radiance upon the West.' Referring to the Revelation of Bahá'u'lláh, he said: 'Erelong will this same light shed a still greater illumination through the potency of the teachings of God . . .'

To elucidate this 'still greater illumination' to the people of the West, 'Abdu'l-Bahá set out in 1911 on his far western journeys. He was

A panel of the exterior ornamentation of the Bahá'í Temple in Wilmette, Illinois, on display in a garden near the Shrine of the Báb

approaching his seventies. A lifetime of harsh treatment and deprivation, of excessive cares and burdens since childhood, had taken its toll upon his physical being. He had had no formal education. He had never given a public address. Yet on a September day in London he graced the pulpit of the City Temple for his first public talk with such dignity and assurance, warmth and kindness radiating from his face, and spoke to an overflowing congregation with such penetrating power and wisdom, as to stir the hearts of all his listeners, learned and unlearned.

'The gift of God to this enlightened age,' he said, 'is the knowledge of the oneness of mankind and of the fundamental oneness of religion. War shall cease between nations, and by the will of God the Most Great Peace shall come; the world will be seen as a new world, and all men will live as brothers.'

He, of all men, sadly knew that the peace of

which he spoke, though assured, was yet to be hard-earned; that the world was not ready to open its heart to this gift; that great wars of unimagined destructiveness must scourge the earth before the sun of peace would rise. Nevertheless, all the prophets had foretold it for millenniums past, and the century of its reality had dawned.

Later, in addressing the New York Peace Society, he was to say, 'The powers of earth cannot withstand the privileges and bestowals which God has ordained for this great and glorious century . . . Man can withstand anything except that which is divinely intended and indicated for the age . . .'

In London and Paris, 'Abdu'l-Bahá spoke on public platforms to large assemblies, in small intimate gatherings, and gave hundreds of interviews to people of both great and lowly stations of life who thronged his door.

'They came from every country in the world!' said Lady Blomfield, in whose London home he resided briefly. 'Every day, all day long, a constant stream . . .'

Now in the spring of 1912 the American Bahá'ís joyously awaited the imminent arrival of the 'Master', as they lovingly called him – a name by which Bahá'u'lláh had taught his followers to address his eldest son. As early as 1898 Western Bahá'ís had journeyed to the Holy Land to visit 'Abdu'l-Bahá, never certain in those precarious times, while he was still a prisoner, of being permitted to see him. There they climbed the long, stone stairway of the house, close by the prison, where 'Abdu'l-Bahá lived. There they remained as his guests, oblivious of the simple fare and accommodation, as the warmth and wisdom of his words, his rare hospitality, and the example of his life, lifted their spirits to a new, unimagined level of reality.

Stairway to Heaven

'It was the "stairway to heaven",' said Carl Scheffler, a young man who accompanied Thornton Chase, first American Bahá'í, on a pilgrimage to the Holy Land in 1907.

The first mention of the Bahá'í Faith in America had been given briefly in a paper read at the World's Parliament of Religions held at the great Columbian Exposition in Chicago in 1893. It was written by a Christian missionary and it quoted a portion of Bahá'u'lláh's interview with Professor Browne of Cambridge. Some five years later a party of fifteen pilgrims hosted by Phoebe Hearst, wife of the late Governor of California and mother of the famed newspaper magnate, arrived in the Holy Land to meet 'Abdu'l-Bahá, then under strict surveillance. The impact of this meeting upon these first pilgrims of the West was profound.

'He is the Most Wonderful Being I have ever

met or ever expect to meet in this world,' Mrs. Hearst recalled later. 'Tho He does not seek to impress one at all, strength, power, purity, love and holiness are radiated from His majestic, yet humble, personality . . .' One member of that party, Mrs. Hearst's butler, Robert Turner, was to become the first black Bahá'í of America.

'It was an amazing experience,' another wrote. 'We four visitors from the Western world felt that our voyage, with all its accompanying inconveniences was a small price to pay for such treasure as we received . . . This began our work . . .[to] acquaint the world with the Message [of Bahá'u'lláh].'

They had done their work well. Everywhere 'Abdu'l-Bahá went in America, as well as in England, throngs of people awaited his coming: some already devoted Bahá'ís, others strongly attracted to the new teachings and to the personality of 'Abdu'l-Bahá of whom they had read, and some with their curiosity piqued.

From coast to coast 'Abdu'l-Bahá traveled ceaselessly for eight months, from April to December, often speaking several times in a single day at meetings, holding countless personal interviews, accessible to all who sought him – and all this time drawing on some hidden spring of the spirit that sustained the prodigal expenditure of his strength and energy.

Volumes have been written about this journey which, like St. Paul's journey to Rome, carried a new Revelation to the West, but unlike that journey was lived almost continuously in the public eye. Records of his public talks given in churches, synagogues, universities, and before societies concerned with peace, philanthropy, science, and philosophy, were later published. Innumerable eyewitness accounts have been recorded of the meetings and personal interviews.

'Abdu'l-Bahá did not seek out the wealthy and powerful, nor would he accept the often freely offered funds for his work. But many distinguished leaders of American life came to him: government officials, diplomats, members of consulates, cabinet members, judges, scientists, educators, and others of renown. Among them were Theodore Roosevelt; the British Ambassador, James Bryce (later Viscount Bryce); Lee McClung, Treasurer of the United States, to name but a few. The last-named, deeply moved by an interview with 'Abdu'l-Bahá, said: 'I seemed to be in the presence of one of the great old prophets – Isaiah–Elijah–Moses . . . No . . . He seemed to me like my Divine Father.'

Alexander Graham Bell, noted inventor, invited him to a gathering held regularly in his home and asked him to address his guests. To Admiral Peary, whose North Pole expedition had recently brought him fame, 'Abdu'l-Bahá said at a meeting in Washington DC: 'I hope you will discover the mysteries of the Kingdom of God.'

Boston, Philadelphia, New York, Cleveland, and other eastern cities were visited, some several times. For the most part newspaper writers were respectful of this teacher from the East and many gave true accounts of his words. The editor of the *Montreal Daily Star* not only published an accurate interview with 'Abdu'l-Bahá, but personally called on him at his residence and later wrote in an editorial: '. . . the universal peace for which he hopes and in which he believes has no resemblance to the fantastic chimera of slack-thinking sophists . . . For 'Abdu'l-Bahá, with all his hatred of war and horror at its moral and material results, has no delusions as to the conditions in Europe today or the trend of political events . . . "A great war in Europe is a certainty . . ."' he quoted 'Abdu'l-Bahá. ' "International peace can only be reached by an international agreement entered

'Abdu'l-Bahá, son of Bahá'u'lláh, appointed by him to be the interpreter and exemplar of his teachings [19]

The home of 'Abdu'l-Bahá in Haifa, after his release from the prison-city of 'Akká

into by all nations." '

In Chicago 'Abdu'l-Bahá spoke at many meetings, met with hundreds of individuals who received from him a new spiritual orientation in their lives. On a May afternoon he laid the cornerstone of the Bahá'í Temple, saying then to those who had undertaken this enormous task: 'The Temple is built.'

The long train journey continued westward: Minneapolis, St. Paul, Omaha, Denver, Salt Lake City – and finally California where he was to spend more than three weeks. Here at Stanford University, Palo Alto, the historic meeting with the University president, Dr David Starr Jordan, took place. Some two thousand university people and community leaders came to hear him give a talk that has been described as 'one of the greatest, most powerful of His ministry'.[15]

In San Francisco, at Temple Emmanu-El, a congregation of similar size heard his moving address on the mission and purpose of all the great Prophets of God. 'The age has dawned when human fellowship will become a reality,' he said in conclusion. 'For all mankind shall dwell in peace and security beneath the shelter of the great tabernacle of the one living God.'

Back in New York on board the SS *Celtic* ready to depart for Europe, he spoke to those assembled to bid him a reluctant farewell from their shores.

'You must be free from prejudice and fanaticism, beholding no differences between the races and religions,' he said. 'Exert yourselves with heart and soul so that perchance through your efforts the light of Universal Peace may shine and this darkness of estrangement and enmity may be dispelled . . . that all men may become as one family and consort together in love and kindness . . . for all are the inhabitants of one

Persian Street in Haifa showing entrance to ʻAbdu'l-Bahá's house

planet, the people of one original nativity and the flocks of one shepherd.'

To those who had been quickened by the spirit he brought, he made this final appeal: 'It is my hope that you may become successful in this high calling, so that like brilliant lamps you may cast light upon the world of humanity . . . unto this I call you, praying to God to strengthen and bless you.' His silvery beard stirred in the wind as he stood on the deck – and then he was gone from their sight.

It has been said that the poet and artist Khalil Gibran received his inspiration for his book, *The Prophet*, from being in ʻAbdu'l-Bahá's presence. Be that as it may, Gibran sketched his portrait and said of him: 'For the first time I saw form noble enough to be the receptacle for Holy Spirit!'

During his return journey to the Holy Land ʻAbdu'l-Bahá again visited London, went to Oxford, and spent several days in Edinburgh. In all these places he was graciously received by people of learning – yet he found time to visit the poor and needy and the orphans. Paris, Stuttgart (and other German towns), Vienna, Budapest, knew his footsteps. Although there were as yet no Bahá'ís residing in Budapest, many interviews were sought by journalists, public talks were requested of him. Among the noted people whom he met were two world-renowned orientalists: Professor Arminius Vambéry and Professor Ignaz Goldziher, the first person of the Jewish Faith to occupy a professorial chair at the University of Budapest.

ʻAbdu'l-Bahá returned to Haifa at the close of 1913 with eight years of his ministry remaining to him. Until the last moment of earthly life, all his waking hours would be spent in service to the Faith of Bahá'u'lláh, and to that 'Most Great Peace' that was the pearl within its shell.

The city of Haifa with its semi-circular bay, by moonlight

14

A DREAM OF
CITIES AND MEN

It was nearly five months before Sarajevo. The Great War foreshadowed in the Tablets of Bahá'u'lláh, and sadly presaged by 'Abdu'l-Bahá on his Western tour, had not yet come, though its rumblings could be heard in the West. One February day 'Abdu'l-Bahá sat at a window gazing intently over the rooftiles of Haifa across the bay to 'Akká, narrowly circumscribed within its walls. In his mind a different picture arose and, in the medium of time, far beyond the Great War and other wars to follow.

'In the future,' he said to those gathered near, 'the distance between 'Akká and Haifa will be built up, and the two cities will join and clasp hands, becoming the two terminal sections of one mighty metropolis.'

His companions, looking out at the scene, saw only the same sleepy, sun-bathed towns separated by a wide plain with a few small sailing vessels in the bay.

'This great semicircular bay,' 'Abdu'l-Bahá continued, 'will be transformed into the finest harbor . . . The great vessels of all peoples will come to this port, bringing on their decks thousands and thousands of men and women from every part of the globe. The mountain and the plain will be dotted with the most modern buildings and palaces. Industries will be established and various institutions of philanthropic nature will be founded.'

His listeners were caught up in his words, trying to visualize the picture that he drew for them.

'The flowers of civilization and culture from all nations will be brought here to blend their fragrances together and blaze the way for the brotherhood of man. Wonderful gardens, orchards, groves and parks will be laid out on all sides.'

Then he added the final brush strokes to his canvas of the future. 'The entire harbor from 'Akká to Haifa will be one path of illumination . . . Mount Carmel itself, from top to bottom, will be submerged in a sea of lights. A person standing on the summit of Mount Carmel, and the passengers of the steamers coming to it, will look upon the most sublime

Across the street from 'Abdu'l-Bahá's home is the former Western pilgrim house, now used for administrative purposes.

and majestic spectacle of the whole world.'

His work continued apace. Many sought his counsel in addition to scores of Bahá'ís who wrote to him or came to the Holy Land. His correspondence was voluminous. More and more he was assisted in his work by his eldest grandson, Shoghi Effendi, whose absolute integrity and deep spiritual insight had been observed and remarked upon by 'Abdu'l-Bahá from the time he was a small lad.

In reply to a letter from Andrew Carnegie, wealthy financier and philanthropist deeply dedicated to the cause of peace, 'Abdu'l-Bahá wrote: 'Today the most important object of the kingdom of God is the promulgation of the cause of universal peace and the principle of the oneness of the world of humanity.'

The Great War came and with it the devastation of lives and nations. It reached beyond Europe and across the sands of Palestine.

'Abdu'l-Bahá, as practical as he was idealistic, had foreseen the coming famine. He planted wheat crops and stored the grain. When the threat of hunger came, he was able to feed the people, especially the poor who faced starvation.

With the war's end, some in Europe remembered 'Abdu'l-Bahá's visit and his admonitions on peace. Though commending their efforts for peace, he declined their invitation to attend the Peace Congress. 'When a conference is convened, representative of all nations and working under the influence of the Word of God, then universal peace will be established.'[16]

In response to the Executive Committee of the Central Organization for a Durable Peace at The Hague, he sent a long message, reiterating the social principles of Bahá'u'lláh as the true foundation of universal peace, based upon the Word of God.

When over seventy, 'Abdu'l-Bahá launched a series of letters to the Bahá'ís of America,

Pilgrim house in the vicinity of the Shrine of the Báb

bestowing upon them the major responsibility for planting the banners of the Faith of Bahá'u'-lláh throughout all continents and islands of the sea. It was called the Divine Plan and Bahá'ís conceive it to be one of his most consequential and far-reaching enterprises. Several arose immediately to travel to the far corners of the earth, though they were a mere rivulet compared to the mighty stream of pioneer teachers who would arise in the future, joined by believers in many lands, long after their Master's passing, long after his pen was stilled.

*   *   *

The skies over Carmel had been grey and somber for days. Now on this late-November morning of 1921 the day dawned radiant and bright, the blue sky mirrored in the sea. By mid-morning multitudes had assembled for the long procession up the slopes of Carmel. It was the funeral of 'Abdu'l-Bahá, and Haifa had never

before witnessed such an event. It was like a scene from some Divine tragedy and indeed countless hearts were stricken – and yet, above the grief, there rose an air of victory. As in life, so in death, 'Abdu'l-Bahá was surrounded by a cross section of humanity he had loved and served so well – rich and poor, learned and unlearned, many races and religions – ten thousand gathered on the Mountain of God in a pageant of farewell to him.

The leaders of Jewish, Christian, Muslim and Druze communities were there to pay tribute. From Jerusalem came the High Commissioner of Palestine with his staff. Several nations were represented by their Consuls and messages poured in from national leaders from near and far. There were Arabs, Greeks, Turks, Armenians, Jews, Egyptians, Kurds, Americans, Europeans. Boy Scout troops marched in the procession. Prayers and chants were heard in many tongues.

'I have never known a more united expression

of regret and respect,' the Governor of Jerusalem later wrote.

The poor wept, remembering not only gifts of food and clothing, but the intangible gifts of cheer and encouragement that had so often lifted their hearts. 'Our father has left us!' they cried.

Before the assembled throng a celebrated Christian writer spoke: 'O 'Abdu'l-Bahá! . . . thou great and generous one! . . . Thou didst bestow life upon us, guided us and taught us. Thou hast lived among us, great, with all that the word greatness means.'

A noted Muslim orator exclaimed: 'Which one of his perfect deeds can I mention to you when they are greater than can be mentioned and more than can be counted! . . . in every heart he has left a glorious trace and on every tongue a beautiful mention.'

The Bishop of the Greek Catholic Church spoke of 'Abdu'l-Bahá's 'remarkable, majestic personality and his matchless philanthropic deeds toward the poor.'

A progressive Jewish leader of Haifa said in a lengthy tribute: 'As to his life, it was the living example of self-sacrifice, preferring the good and the welfare of others to his own. Blessed are those who were near him, for they have read in him the greatest page of religious and social philosophy . . . 'Abdu'l-Bahá, and before him Bahá'u'lláh, have carried on their shoulders this glorious work – the establishment of universal peace . . .'

'Does it seem,' he concluded, 'that there is a divine wisdom in all these affairs in specializing the Holy Land to be, as it always has been and always shall be, the source of higher and more spiritual idealism?'[17]

These are but a sampling of the outpourings from those who, though followers of other religions, saw in 'Abdu'l-Bahá the 'living example' of all that men of goodwill work and yearn for on earth.

Newspaper representatives from many lands attended the funeral. Stated the London *Morning Post*: 'At his table Buddhist and Mohammedan, Hindu and Zoroastrian, Jew and Christian, sat in amity.'

The *New York World* cited a report written some months before by their special correspondent who had visited 'Abdu'l-Bahá in the Holy Land: 'Having once looked upon 'Abdu'l-Baha, his personality is indelibly impressed upon the mind: the majestic, venerable figure clad in the flowing aba, his head crowned with a turban white as his head and hair; the piercing deep set eyes whose glances shake the heart; the smile that pours its sweetness over all.'

The New York *Evening Telegram* recalled his visit of some years before: 'Churches of all denominations in New York city and Chicago were thrown open to him for, unlike the leaders of many cults, he preached not the errors of present religions but their sameness.' Newspapers in Egypt, India and other parts of the world wrote in equally high appreciation of the personality, character, and work of 'Abdu'l-Bahá, and numerous cables poured in from world leaders.

What of the Bahá'ís? What of the followers of the Faith of Bahá'u'lláh, now scattered in communities in many parts of the world, struggling to fulfill 'Abdu'l-Bahá's bidding – to carry the message of the oneness of God and of His Messengers, and the oneness of all mankind, to the far corners of the earth? *Where would they turn?* Were they now leaderless with only a faint pattern of the administrative structure designed by Bahá'u'lláh yet visible? Would the unity which was the cornerstone of their Faith, preserved by 'Abdu'l-Bahá for thirty years against many attempts to tear it asunder, now weaken and fade away?

There was no need to fear. 'Abdu'l-Bahá's greatest gift to the Bahá'í world was about to be manifested in a written document, a Will and Testament signed and sealed by his own hand. In it he named Shoghi Effendi, great-grandson of Bahá'u'lláh, and now a young man of twenty-four, as the Guardian of the Bahá'í Faith, the one to whom all should turn, the interpreter of the revealed words. In Shoghi Effendi, 'Abdu'l-Bahá assured the Bahá'ís, they would find the vision, the gift of leadership, and the purity of spirit to preserve the unity and integrity of their Faith. He would guide them to high plateaus of achievement far beyond their present realization and hope.

House in the shadow of the prison in 'Akká where 'Abdu'l-Bahá resided before transferring his residence to Haifa

Obelisk marking the site of a future Bahá'í temple on top of Mount Carmel

15

THE MASTER DESIGNER

Shoghi Effendi had grown up in the home of 'Abdu'l-Bahá. He had been shaped and guided by him and the love they bore for each other was deep and abiding. And yet, outside this bond, Shoghi Effendi had demonstrated from earliest childhood a devotion to the Faith of Bahá'u'lláh that was beyond his close filial attachment to his beloved grandfather. Proficient in several languages, he had served 'Abdu'l-Bahá as secretary and interpreter for some years. Even now he was attending Oxford University in order to perfect himself in English, as was 'Abdu'l-Bahá's wish.

The new young Guardian returned to the Holy Land to shoulder the enormous task of guiding the community of Bahá'ís, now scattered about the five continents, into the world religion it was destined to become. Soon the Bahá'ís were abundantly aware of the priceless gift bestowed upon them. Shoghi Effendi was their Guardian, the appointed leader of their Faith – but he was also a comrade in service, their 'true brother', as he signed his letters to them. Under his patient but zealous leadership they began to arise in ever greater numbers to carry the 'glad-tidings' of Bahá'u'lláh's message of peace to 'every spot on the surface of the earth, and . . . to each one of its cities'.

It devolved upon Shoghi Effendi to transmit the dream and prophecy into visible reality. He was the 'master designer', the one who could envision the end from the beginning. It was he who raised the superstructure of the Shrine of the Báb; who built the classical Greek-styled Archives Building nestled into the side of the mountain; who chose the site for the majestic headquarters of the Universal House of Justice. Just below on the rising slope he created a memorial garden of tranquil beauty as the final resting-place for members of 'Abdu'l-Bahá's family.

The work went slowly at first – a new terrace added, gardens and paths laid out, an ornamental gate placed. In addition to refurbishing Bahá'u'lláh's room at Bahjí and making it a place of visitation for Bahá'ís, the entire Mansion was rehabilitated and restored to its original beauty. Then, with his unerring taste, Shoghi Effendi

made it a focal point where evidences and tokens of the work of Bahá'u'lláh and his followers could be viewed. The expansive central hall and other rooms were used to display historical photographs of believers and their exploits throughout the world, along with documents tracing the progress of the Bahá'í Faith. Multitudes of Bahá'í books in many languages, carpets, paintings and other ornaments, added warmth and charm. The area surrounding the Mansion and the adjoining Shrine of Bahá'u'lláh was greatly expanded and made to submit to a magnificent scheme of landscape architecture.

The development and beautification of the World Center in the Holy Land was only one of

Steps of the International Archives Building

One of the gardens of the Shrine of the Báb

the far-reaching objectives which Shoghi
Effendi set out to achieve. From the start of his
ministry he began the prodigious task of lifting
the Bahá'í Faith from the obscurity in which it
was still largely ensconced to its recognition as
an independent world religion – a religion with
a holy Scripture, laws, institutions, and an
administrative structure uniquely its own.

Shoghi Effendi's task was enormous. Countless letters were written, filled with vision and
hope, guiding, educating, inspiring, and stimu-
lating the Bahá'ís to rise and take up their
challenge to fulfill Bahá'u'lláh's 'great purpose
for mankind'. The Great War had ended only a

Gardens at Bahjí

few years before. Its bitter disappointment and suffering had, the Guardian wrote, 'stirred deeply the conscience of mankind, and opened the eyes of an unbelieving world to the Power of the Spirit that alone can cure its sicknesses, heal its wounds, and establish the long-promised reign of undisturbed prosperity and peace.'

Some of Shoghi Effendi's letters to the Bahá'ís of the world were in the nature of brilliant expositions on world conditions that came to be known as his World Order Letters. Therein he analyzed the titanic social upheaval taking place throughout the world in all areas of human life as peoples and nations struggled toward the 'coming of age of the entire human race'. He gave an illuminating glimpse of the world of the future – a universal civilization to which all humanity, be it unknowingly, was being inexorably propelled:

'The coming of age of the entire human race [will] be proclaimed and celebrated by all the peoples and nations of the earth,' he wrote. A 'world civilization [will] be born, flourish, and perpetuate itself, a civilization with a fullness of life such as the world has never seen nor can as yet conceive ... Then will the promise enshrined in all the Books of God be redeemed, and all the prophecies uttered by the Prophets of old come to pass, and the vision of seers and poets be realized.'

Shoghi Effendi's high vision, coupled with his indefatigable energy and zeal, galvanized the Bahá'ís into action. Often he likened them to a spiritual army, an 'army of light', that they might acquire the discipline and the will to victory. Their chief 'ammunition', however, was the example of their lives as lived day by day among their fellowmen. He cautioned them to exhibit 'a high sense of moral rectitude in their social and administrative activities', along with 'complete freedom from prejudice in their deal-ings with peoples of a different race, class, creed, or color.'

The mantle 'Abdu'l-Bahá had placed upon Shoghi Effendi included the function of inter-pretation of the Bahá'í writings. He was quick to see that the expansion of the Faith throughout the world depended upon each Bahá'í of every nation, tribe, or tongue having the sacred writings of his Faith published in his own language. This was a religion in which *each* believer was urged to study for himself. Each was urged to contribute his own best thought to those consultative bodies (Spiritual Assemblies) which he himself had helped to elect, and from whose deliberations guidance evolved for the entire community of believers.

Soon many of the major writings of Bahá'u'-lláh and the interpretations of 'Abdu'l-Bahá began to appear in printed form in a number of languages. This alchemy had its beginning in the matchless English translations made by Shoghi Effendi, which in turn became the basis for translation into French, German, Spanish, Ital-ian, and other languages. Within a decade the bibliography of Bahá'í literature included not only all the European languages but most major Oriental tongues as well. Journals, magazines, pamphlets emerged and the works of an increas-ing number of Bahá'í authors were published. During the thirty-six years of Shoghi Effendi's ministry a veritable explosion of Bahá'í pub-lished works occurred. Its shower of sparks continued to spread outward into a multitude of tribal tongues and vernaculars, so that by 1981 the Teachings of the Bahá'í Faith could be read in more than 660 languages!

In addition to his own prodigious outpouring of translations and original writings, and his constant guidance to struggling Bahá'í com-munities in varying stages of growth around the world, Shoghi Effendi set in motion systematic plans for the expansion of the Bahá'í community and its administrative institutions throughout all continents of the globe. Its fundamental administrative structure had been established in the writings of Bahá'u'lláh and further delineated by 'Abdu'l-Bahá. They did not leave man to himself – to ponder, innovate, and eventually create division within the ranks. Bahá'u'lláh's Will and Testament, written by his own hand, as well as that of his appointed successor, 'Abdu'l-Bahá, made unique, firmly fixed provisions to maintain the unity and wholeness of the Bahá'í community in all its diversity, and to keep its Scripture pure and unadulterated. Attempts at disruption were made, both from the outside and from a few disaffected members seeking personal leadership and power, but all came to naught.

In 1953 Shoghi Effendi launched a ten-year plan calling for widespread expansion of the Faith on a global scale. To the Bahá'ís of that time the plan seemed more dream than possible deed. But their Guardian called them to four large intercontinental conferences around the world where they gathered to consult upon the plans and to marshal their forces. The call was raised for 'pioneer' teachers and soon individuals and whole families arose to go forth and plant the banners of their Faith in new lands. They went not as paid missionaries but as volunteer teachers re-establishing their lives and their livelihood. Sometimes these fledgling pioneers on their way to their posts would find themselves as guests at Shoghi Effendi's table in Haifa; often they came later as pilgrims to share their first victories.

Shoghi Effendi did not live to see the completion of his great plan although he witnessed it well on its way to complete success. In November of 1957 while visiting London he suddenly passed away. Everywhere Bahá'ís were stunned and heartbroken. Yet when the first shock and grief subsided, they arose courageously, determined to bring complete victory to their loved Guardian's plan.

At the conclusion of the plan, in April of 1963, nearly seven thousand Bahá'ís gathered in the Royal Albert Hall in London to celebrate their achievements, and to mark the hundredth anniversary of Bahá'u'lláh's declaration of his Mission. Planeload after planeload they came, from all over the planet. The firstfruits of their labors were visible on every hand – in the blend of races and nationalities; in the tribal dress of African Bahá'ís, the colorful costumes of Latin American Indians, in the Oriental saris and robes. Even the Aboriginals from Australia were represented. It was the 'family of man' and the London press bore witness to the extraordinary jubilance of this gathering of the human race.

The high point of this great jubilee was the presence of the nine members of the newly-formed Universal House of Justice. It had just been elected a few days before the conference by members of fifty-six national administrative bodies at the historic first international convention of the Bahá'í Faith in Haifa.*

Reverently they assembled, thousands in relays, at the grave of Shoghi Effendi in London, their hearts overflowing with thanksgiving for the inspired leadership of their beloved Guardian who had brought them to this point. Even the jubilee itself had been chosen by him, a gift and a reward from a 'true brother'. Later when they left the joyous gathering, their hearts were confident under the leadership of their Universal House of Justice, the supreme institution ordained by Bahá'u'lláh.

* In 1978 at the fourth international convention in Haifa, members of 122 national administrative bodies participated in the election of the Universal House of Justice.

16

A CROWN
OF BEAUTY

Although 'Abdu'l-Bahá's glorious prophecy of a lasting world peace is not yet fulfilled, much of his vision of Carmel and the cities on the Bay has been realized. Today Haifa's busy port harbors the ships of many lands, and the small, sleepy village has grown into a large, modern city supporting numerous industries. At night a panorama of lights reaches from the mountain-top and forms a necklace around the Bay to 'Akká.

The 'wonderful gardens, . . . groves and parks' of 'Abdu'l-Bahá's word picture adorn the slopes of Carmel, once desolate with rock and thorn. The golden dome of the Shrine of the Báb rises like a 'crown of beauty' in their midst.

'It is one of the most conspicuous structures on Mount Carmel, catching the eye from any part of town, or even from far out at sea,' wrote Carl Alpert of the Haifa Technion some years ago in an article entitled 'Another Religion Calls Israel Home'.[18] Other stately structures have risen nearby to form the world administrative center of the Bahá'í Faith. High on the point of Carmel that looks toward the Valley of Sharon and juts out to the sea is a tall obelisk that marks the site of a future Bahá'í House of Worship.

The gardens on Carmel as well as those surrounding Bahjí near 'Akká are beauty spots of the East, known around the world. They attract an ever-widening throng of visitors, Bahá'í pilgrims and others, from all over the globe.

'After having visited many of the famous gardens on the continent of Europe and in England,' wrote Robert McLaughlin, Dean (Emeritus) of Princeton's School of Architecture, 'I find the Bahá'í gardens at Bahjí and on Mount Carmel the most beautiful of all. There one is lifted into another world.'

'Where do the funds come from?'

It is a question frequently asked by visitors at the Bahá'í World Center as well as at Bahá'í temples around the world. It is a question Bahá'ís love to answer. Sometimes visitors look for donation boxes or some place to offer a gift of money to show their appreciation for the work of the Bahá'ís. There are no donation boxes, no collection plates, no financial drives to

solicit funds from the public. Donations are not accepted from visitors to these places, though all are welcome to come, to pray, and be refreshed by their beauty and peace.

A distinguishing feature of the Bahá'í Faith is the principle that financial contributions for the work of the Faith are accepted only from members; 'contributing to the funds of the Faith', the Universal House of Justice has stated, 'is a . . . privilege of profound significance . . . ', a special privilege for Bahá'ís only.

It is a privilege Bahá'ís keenly value. The creation of these sacred places open to people of all racial, religious, and cultural backgrounds, is their gift to the world. Like a jewel wrapped in a silken mantle, it is a gift within a gift, a place where the heart may be kindled with new hope for the peace so long foretold by the Prophets.

From the day of Bahá'u'lláh's arrival on these shores, and long before, the hand of God, Bahá'ís believe, was turning and shaping this Spot for its predestined purpose, and in accord with prophecies of old. Although it would take decades to become manifest, Bahá'u'lláh, in the latter years of his life, declared Carmel to be the seat of the Universal House of Justice as well as the site of the sacred Shrine of his Herald and Forerunner, the Báb.

'He, verily, loveth the spot . . . which His footsteps have trodden, . . . from which He raised His call, and upon which He shed His tears.' Thus did Bahá'u'lláh exalt this hallowed place.

During Bahá'u'lláh's sojourn in 'Akká and its environs no Western pilgrims sought his presence. His Faith had not yet been established in the West, although it had aroused the attention and interest of such scholars as E. G. Browne, and the great Russian, Count Leo Tolstoy, who wrote that Bahá'u'lláh's writings 'present us with the highest and purest form of religious teaching'. With the turn of the century came the first pilgrims from the West, opening as it were a gateway for 'Abdu'l-Bahá's extensive European and American travels. Upon his return to the Holy Land the visits from both East and West increased. During Shoghi Effendi's thirty-six-year Guardianship of the Bahá'í Faith, the stream of pilgrims began to widen, halted only by the Second World War and the intermittent persecution of the Bahá'ís in the land of its birth.

Following Shoghi Effendi's worldwide teaching plan and the establishment of the Universal House of Justice in 1963, the doors of expansion opened widely for the Bahá'í Faith, followed by ever-increasing numbers of pilgrims to the Holy Land. Again, alas, in 1979 the fires of persecution once more engulfed the followers of Bahá'u'lláh in the land of his birth, sending many innocent people to death. Yet, like water poured on flames of a sea of oil, the flood of tribulation has served to spread the flames farther abroad. Perhaps nothing in the stirring and eventful history of the Bahá'í Faith since its inception has so alerted just and free nations of the world, not only to the plight of a beleaguered people, but to the principles for which they stand and for which they are willing to die.

Thus a Faith believed to have been silenced by a firing squad in Tabríz and obscured by the walls of a prison cell in 'Akká has continued to burgeon, its leaves and branches reaching throughout the planet, awakening everywhere the ancient dream of the Fatherhood of God and the brotherhood of man that has long slumbered but never died in the hearts of men.

As the paths that radiate outward from the Shrine of Bahá'u'lláh at Bahjí point to the infinite horizon, so does guidance and inspiration continue to radiate from this hallowed place to thousands of Bahá'í communities around the world. And for every Bahá'í, wherever he may abide, the paths are retraced back again to this sacred Spot – for it is a spiritual lodestar that forever beckons him to these shores.

Aerial view of the gardens at Bahjí surrounding the Shrine of Bahá'u'lláh

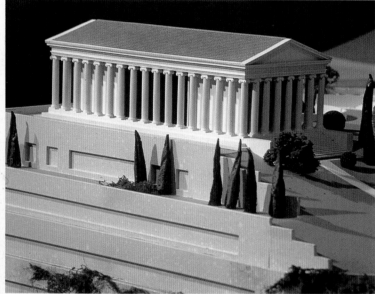

'This beautiful and majestic path, which extends from the Shrine of the Báb to the City of Haifa in line with the greatest avenue of that blessed city, which is adorned with trees and verdant plants and illumined with bright lights, which is the object of the admiration of the people of this region and a source of joy and pride to the authorities in this land, will subsequently be converted, as foreshadowed by the Centre of the Covenant, into the Highway of the Kings and Rulers of the World.

'These mighty embodiments of kingly power, humble pilgrims to the Sanctuary of the Lord, will, upon their arrival in the Holy Land, first proceed to the Plain of 'Akká, there to visit and circumambulate the Qiblih of the people of Bahá, the Point around which circle in adoration the Concourse on High. They will then make their way to this august and venerated city, and climb the slopes of Mount Carmel. With the utmost rapture, ardour and devotion, they will hasten towards this Sacred Spot and, with reverence and submissiveness, humility and lowliness, ascend these terraces to approach the luminous precincts of the sanctified and holy Shrine. Reaching the threshold of the Sanctuary of Grandeur, they will cast their crowns upon the ground, prostrate themselves to kiss its fragrant earth and, circling around its hallowed arcade, call out "Here am I, Here am I, O Thou Who art the Exalted, the Most Exalted One!," and recite in tones of fervent supplication the perspicuous Verses of the Tablet of Carmel.'

Shoghi Effendi

Models for the building projects on Mount Carmel to be realized in the 1990s. From the top: the International Teaching Centre; the International Bahá'í Library; the Centre for the Study of the Texts. Opposite: the Terraces above and below the Shrine of the Báb, extending from the foot to the ridge of the mountain.

'The cities of Haifa and 'Akká will be as one city, by being built up, and the plains between the two will be transformed into gardens, groves, and most magnificent buildings. A vast, well built, smooth, adorned avenue, in the utmost beauty and delicacy, will be extended from Mount Carmel to Bahjí, and tall and pleasant trees will provide their shade over it, thus adding to the purity and freshness of the air. A great port will be built in this sea, in order to enable large ships to approach the land and to bring their passengers easily to shore. The heads and rulers of the various nations will come in groups. Electric lights will turn the dark nights into a vast stretch of light. 'Akká and Haifa will become a great centre for institutes, and the dawning place for the light of sciences and crafts. At the foot of this great blessed Mount Carmel, will reside scholars and great thinkers of the world. 'Akká and Haifa will become the means of the life of the world and the education of the peoples' new generations.'

From a talk given by 'Abdu'l-Bahá in Haifa, 1919

REFERENCES

1. Dr Ugo Giachery *Shoghi Effendi, Recollections* (George Ronald, London, 1973), p. 65.

2. Isaiah 45:1 (Rev. Std. Vers.)

3. George Townshend, Introduction to Nabíl *The Dawn-Breakers* (Bahá'í Publishing Trust, Wilmette, Illinois, 1932), p. xxiii.

4. Nabíl *The Dawn-Breakers* (see above), p. 92.

5. E. G. Browne *A Persian Anthology*, ed. E. Denison Ross (London, 1927), p. 72.

6. E. G. Browne (ed.) *A Traveller's Narrative* (Cambridge University Press, 1891), Notes p.309.

7. These words have been set to music by Charles Wolcott (former musical director of Metro-Goldwyn-Mayer and Walt Disney Studios), arranged for both solo and choral versions. It has been recorded by Norman Bailey, London L'oiseau-Lyre, Decca, London.

8. For the full text of this extraordinary interview and its effect upon Professor Browne, see J. E. Esslemont *Bahá'u'lláh and the New Era* 4th rev. edn (Bahá'í Publishing Trust, Wilmette, Illinois, 1976), pp. 52–3.

9. H. M. Balyuzi *Bahá'u'lláh, The King of Glory* (George Ronald, Oxford, 1980), p. 362.

10. Dr David Starr Jordan, President of Stanford University, Palo Alto, California, October 1912.

11. Egyptian *Gazette*, 24 September 1913, quoted in *The Bahá'í World* Vol. XII, p. 623.

12. H. M. Balyuzi *Bahá'u'lláh, The King of Glory* (George Ronald, Oxford, 1980), p. 221. See also p. ix concerning reported words of Bahá'u'lláh.

13. These brief excerpts are taken from Tablets found in *The Proclamation of Bahá'u'lláh* (Bahá'í World Center, Haifa, Israel, 1967), and are quoted in numerous books including Shoghi Effendi *The Promised Day is Come* (Bahá'í Publishing Trust, Wilmette, Illinois, 1980).

14. Mark Twain (Samuel Clemens) *The Innocents Abroad* (New York and London, 1869).

15. H. M. Balyuzi *'Abdu'l-Bahá* (George Ronald, Oxford, 1971), p. 288. Many of the statements quoted in this description of 'Abdu'l-Bahá's travels in America are given in Mr Balyuzi's book.

16. *Selections from the Writings of 'Abdu'l-Bahá* (Bahá'í World Centre, Haifa, 1978), p. 296.

17. *Star of the West*. The Bahá'í Magazine Vol. XII, pp. 261–6. Reprinted in *Star of the West* Vol. 7 (George Ronald, Oxford, 1978).

18. *The Reconstructionist* Vol. XXI, No. 6, 19 April 1955 (Jewish Reconstructionist Foundation, Inc., New York City).

19. From a colour photograph of 'Abdu'l-Bahá made by Nadar in Paris in 1911. The original plate was recently acquired by M. Francis Delvert and full reproduction rights have been given by him to his relatives and to the Bahá'í Faith.

A SHORT READING LIST

Bahá'í Scripture and Basic Texts

BAHÁ'U'LLÁH. *Gleanings from the Writings of Bahá'u'-lláh*. Trans. by Shoghi Effendi. Wilmette, Illinois: Bahá'í Publishing Trust, 2nd rev. edn 1976.

——*The Proclamation of Bahá'u'lláh*. Haifa: Bahá'í World Centre, 1967.

'ABDU'L-BAHÁ. *Foundations of World Unity*. Wilmette, Illinois: Bahá'í Publishing Trust, 1971.

——*Paris Talks*. London: Bahá'í Publishing Trust, 11th edn 1969.

——*Some Answered Questions*. A series of table talks on a wide variety of topics. Wilmette, Illinois: Bahá'í Publishing Trust, 1981.

SHOGHI EFFENDI. *Call to the Nations*. Extracts from his statements on World Order. Haifa: Bahá'í World Centre, 1977.

——*God Passes By*. A history of the first century of the Bahá'í Faith. Wilmette, Illinois: Bahá'í Publishing Trust, 1965.

Biographies of the Three Central Figures

BALYUZI, H. M. *Bahá'u'lláh, The King of Glory*. Oxford: George Ronald, 1980.

——*The Báb, The Herald of the Day of Days*. Oxford: George Ronald, 1974.

——*'Abdu'l-Bahá, The Centre of the Covenant of Bahá'u'lláh*. Oxford: George Ronald, 1973.

Introductory Books

BRAUN, EUNICE. *From Strength to Strength*. The First Half Century of the Formative Age of the Bahá'í Era (1921–1971, but including to 1973). Wilmette, Illinois: Bahá'í Publishing Trust, 1978.

ESSLEMONT, J. E. *Bahá'u'lláh and the New Era*. An introduction to the history and teachings of the Bahá'í Faith, available in many languages. Wilmette, Illinois: Bahá'í Publishing Trust, 4th rev. edn 1975.

HOFMAN, DAVID. *The Renewal of Civilization*. A brief account of the history and teachings. Oxford: George Ronald, 1981.

HOLLEY, HORACE. *Religion for Mankind*. Essays on world religion as the progenitor of world order and world peace. Oxford: George Ronald, 1976.

HUDDLESTON, JOHN. *The Earth Is But One Country*. An analysis of the needs of mankind today, and how the Bahá'í Faith is contributing to the growth of a world-wide civilization. London: Bahá'í Publishing Trust, 1976.

TOWNSHEND, GEORGE. *The Promise of All Ages*. An introduction to the Bahá'í Faith of particular significance for Christians.

Most of these titles are available in public and university libraries, or may be ordered from bookshops or directly from the publishers.